William Sidney Rossiter

An Accidental Romance

And Ohter Stories

William Sidney Rossiter

An Accidental Romance
And Ohter Stories

ISBN/EAN: 9783744692687

Printed in Europe, USA, Canada, Australia, Japan

Cover: Foto ©Thomas Meinert / pixelio.de

More available books at **www.hansebooks.com**

An Accidental Romance,
and Other Stories

William Sidney Rossiter

New York
The Republic Press
14 Lafayette Place
1895

Preface

THERE are no red lights in the pages which follow—no literary rockets, no cattails dipped in kerosene and lighted "to mark the path of progress," no morals pointed, no isms illumined.

This little book has only one excuse for existence. The stories it contains were written to divert the author's thoughts from pressing daily cares, for the habit of the pen, once acquired in newspaper work, never can be entirely overcome.

If, by passing these sketches along, he can please or divert some other member of the toiling, anxious human family, he is content. Possibly some more pretentious brother who points a moral or lights an ism, does not accomplish even as much. Who knows ?

Contents

An Accidental Romance.

The American Association for the Advancement of Invention had held its annual meeting
in Denver. The sessions lasted three days, and
they had been largely attended and marked by
great enthusiasm and many brilliant and schol-
arly addresses. After the election of officers
and final adjournment a large number of the
members decided to make a trip to Pike's Peak
before separating. I hailed this excursion as
a welcome respite from official cares, for I was
third vice-president of the association (to which
office I had just been re-elected), and I had been
occupied constantly with important official
duties during the sessions. It was, therefore,
with a delightful sense of freedom that I joined
my fellow-members in making up the jolliest
party, I am inclined to believe, that ever ascend-
ed Colorado's famous mountain. Of course I did
not realize how deeply that brief trip would

affect all my future life; but then, nobody ever does realize. The realizing business is all transacted in retrospection.

We had reached the summit, and I was standing with a group of friends looking off on that stupendous panorama of lake and mountain, when Major D. Pringle Whitehouse, of Jersey City, a former corresponding secretary of the association, and widely known as the inventor of an improved automatic cork ejector, tapped me on the shoulder.

"You're going directly East, aren't you, Dunkley?" he inquired.

"I expect to," I replied.

"Do me a big favor, won't you? Take my umbrella back with you, and keep it till I call for it. I've just decided to 'do' California with Reed and MacSimmons. Can't rustle around the land of sunshine with a family umbrella, you know. Give me away completely. Haven't time to pack it and hunt up an express office. Haven't even time to ship it. Help me out, won't you, my boy?"

I murmured something about a willingness to oblige, which I was far from feeling.

"I knew you would," he continued. "Don't let it bother you, but don't lose it, whatever you do—that umbrella, sir, was my only inheritance from my Great Uncle Williams. It's thirty-four years old if it's a day. I should be heartbroken

If I lost it, Dunkley, so hang on to it tightly. Great mark of esteem, in fact, to select you to care for it. So long. See you in New York."

So saying, he pressed into my reluctant hand a huge black silk umbrella, with a carved ivory handle representing a bunch of grapes and two cupids rampant, nodded reassuringly, and was gone.

This development was as sudden as it was unwelcome. I had come upon the excursion as a relief from official cares, and here I stood on the snowclad summit of Pike's Peak, Colorado, looking off upon the headwaters of four great rivers, upon mountain, lake and forest, and Colorado lying like a map below, clasping "Great Uncle Williams's" family umbrella, and charged with its safe conduct for a couple of thousand miles.

I think I could have claimed reasonably to be as kindly and accommodating as the average bachelor of thirty-seven years. I ought to have been. I had a good disposition, was sound of mind and body, and had had a prosperous and rather uneventful career, but I abhorred favors and commissions. I do not refer to cash commissions; doubtless they are different. My experience with that sort is limited. The antipathy I felt to other people's errands, however, dated, I believe, from a distressing experience in my childhood, which was deeply impressed upon me, both internally and externally. Our nextdoor neighbor, an elderly and vastly particular spinster, named Wegan, had commissioned me to mail a letter for her, which, boylike, I completely forgot to do, and when she asked me, two weeks later, what I had done with that letter, I searched in every pocket and solemnly declared I had mailed it; as, indeed, I thought I must have done. A month afterward I discovered the letter in another jacket, and I still recall the horror I experienced upon finding it. There was but one thing to do. I mailed it, and waited for the consequences with many misgivings. Two days passed and I breathed easier, but the third morning I was awakened by a hammering in our neighbor's backyard. I opened the window cautiously, and saw two carpenters at work and a third man unloading lumber. On the back porch stood old Miss Wegan, in a red wrapper and curl papers, and a halo of excitement.

"Go away, men," she called.

The carpenters looked a good deal surprised.

"It's all right," said one of them, reassuringly.

"What's all right?"

"About the henhouse."

"What henhouse?"

"Old Miss Wegan's."

"Old Miss Wegan don't want any henhouse."

"Yes she does."

"No she don't."

"Mr. Gibbons had a letter from her ordering a henhouse put up immediately, and we're here doin' it."

"He never got the letter," said the owner of the curl papers, emphatically.

"Yes, he did. He says to tell you he can't get the corrugated roosts till next week."

"I don't want any roosts."

"And the cupola is to have a weather-vane on it."

"I don't want any cupola," repeated Miss Wegan, desperately. "I don't want any henhouse at all. I ordered one two months ago, but the letter was lost in the mail, and it got so late I sold my chickens. That's the end of it. Now, go away, all of you," she added in no pleasant tones.

"Can't ma'am; we've come to build a henhouse, and we're goin' to. The order only came yesterday, but the lumber's cut a'ready."

I felt a cold chill run down my youthful spine.

"Yesterday?" repeated Miss Wegan in surprise. "It's that horrid, careless Dunkley boy," she said. "He shall hear of this."

I had heard of it already. I closed the window, jumped into my clothes and hurried downstairs.

"Ma," I said, "may I spend the day down at the Centre?"

It was a useless device. It merely delayed

the reckoning. The case in hand, however, did not call for reminiscence, or a dissertation on predilections or antipathies. Here I was on Pike's Peak (fact one), constituted keeper and custodian of Great Uncle Williams's umbrella, and the umbrella was at that moment burdening me (fact two.)

"Did you ever see such an imposition?" I exclaimed, irritably, to Randall, who was next to me. "The man concludes to go to California; he doesn't want to bother with his unsightly old umbrella, so he shoves it into the hands of the first man his eyes light upon, and says: 'There, take that to New York for me, and mind you don't lose it.' Such unlimited cheek," I added, wrathfully, "ought to be converted into horse-power."

"It's a shame," said Randall, sympathetically. "You've had enough to do to deserve a rest. Let me have that umbrella, and when I get back to Denver I'll pack it in with some belongings of mine, and ship it East without worrying anybody."

I protested that I had better shoulder the trouble myself, and that I certainly did not wish to take my turn in imposing on a friend —but Randall was firm. He declared that I had done my share, and by relieving me he could aid in a small way the cause of the American Association for the Advancement of Inven-

tion, which we all had so deeply at heart. He
was so much in earnest that I yielded, and
turned over to him with many apologies the
Major's ancestral umbrella, adorned with its
ugly cupids, cautioning him to send it around to
my office in New York at his convenience, and
once more devoted myself to the full enjoyment
of the trip.

On returning to Denver I started East with
as little delay as possible, and all thought of the
Major's umbrella had faded completely from my
mind, due, no doubt, to the fact that I did not
again see Randall, as the members scattered
immediately after the excursion. Five weeks
elapsed—exceedingly busy ones for me, as my
firm was testing a new and remarkable invention that had been described at the Denver meeting, and I was deeply concerned in the results.
Looking up from my desk one afternoon in
August I saw the familiar form of Major D.
Pringle Whitehouse in the doorway. A vague
feeling came over me that there was some reason why I did not want to see Whitehouse, but
I could not recall what it was, and I greeted him
cordially.

"We had a great meeting, didn't we, Dunkley?" he said, as he shook hands and took the
chair I proffered him. "I suppose I am about
the last straggler to get back," he added.

"Where have you been?" I asked.

"Why, to California," he said, looking surprised; "you know I told you when we were up on Pike's Peak that I was going to California with Reed and MacSimmons. I was sorry enough afterward that I left my umbrella behind, for it seemed as though it rained every day till we got to 'Frisco."

It all flashed over me. The Major had turned his umbrella over to me up on the Peak, and now he had come to demand his own. What should I do? I had given it to that confounded Randall; he had not sent the umbrella back to me, and the day before I had heard that there was sickness in his family and that he had gone to the Catskills for a couple of weeks. Doubtless he had brought the Major's umbrella East with him in a packing-case and had not opened it (for if he had, the umbrella would have reached me.) Randall lived in New Jersey, and probably at that very moment Great Uncle What's-His-Name's umbrella was lying boxed up in a case in the cellar of Randall's house, somewhere in Brick Church or All the Oranges. In any event, I must gain time, so I asked the Major about California in general. He talked twenty minutes, and when he showed symptoms of verbal drouth I inquired about a new invention for watering the streets of San Diego. That was good for ten minutes—during which I concluded I had better own up, for the fact must come out ultimately, anyway; so I asked no further questions, and at length the Major veered around to Pike's Peak again.

"I've often thought I imposed on you up there," he said.

"Not at all, Major," I answered, briskly.

"So I dropped in as soon as I got back to apologize and relieve you of your charge."

"Hasn't bothered me a bit," I said, "for I haven't got it down here."

"Not lost?" ejaculated the Major.

"Oh, no. Randall packed it with some things of his own, and brought it back from Denver with him. He has forgotten to send it over, but if you had only dropped me a line before you came in I would have had it here for you."

The Major stroked his beard, which ran in hairy undulations down to his lowest waistcoat button, and looked solicitous.

"I don't know about Randall," he said, doubtfully. "He's flighty. Shouldn't have trusted him myself. Thought I knew you, and what you said could be relied on."

I found myself growing uncomfortable.

"Suppose," I thought, "just suppose, anything should have happened to that umbrella, how could I face my hirsute friend?"

Oh, it's all right," I said, cheerily. "Randall's a first-rate fellow, and as he had some traps to bring East, that umbrella came with them, and is over at his house now, I suppose."

"Traps?" inquired Major Whitehouse, with some interest. "What kind of traps?"

"Household stuff and all that. You know he once lived in Denver."

"Thought you meant rat traps," said the Major, the interest fading out. "I have invented a pneumatic trap, and I am working up a paper to read at the next annual meeting of our association, upon 'The Trap in All ages.' I am tracing the subject from the old wooden skewers of the ancients down to the latest thing in the line, my pneumatic trap. Fascinating subject, sir, fascinating." The Major rose to go.

"Now, Dunkley," he said, "don't forget that umbrella, my boy. It belonged to my Great Uncle Williams, and was all he left out of an ample estate. I wouldn't lose it for a farm—for several large farms."

Saying which, Major D. Pringle Whitehouse departed, to my infinite relief. The afternoon was young and full of possibilities when he entered. It was wrecked and broken and fragmentary when he left. Before I had closed my desk that evening, however, I had written this note:

My Dear Randall:—

The whiskered form of D. Pringle Whitehouse loomed up this afternoon in my office. He demanded his Great Uncle's umbrella, which

I had completely forgotten. You recollect he shoved it into my hands up on Pike's Peak last month, and asked me to be a father to it while he was in California. I hadn't thought of it from that day to this, but it all came back to me, and I told him you had kindly brought it back to New York in a packing case you were conveying home, and that doubtless at that very historic moment, Great Uncle Williams's umbrella lay in a box over in Brick Church or All the Oranges. This box business is a delicate emulation of the pious example set by Great Uncle Williams himself, which I should like to see encouraged, for he has occupied a box for twenty-nine years, and apparently "stays put." However, the Major must have his umbrella. He was pleasant but persistent, so I beg of you if the family is away and the house shut, to hie you to Brick Church, or Orange Centre, or Orange Phosphate, and produce that umbrella. Don't take any chances on the packing case. Buy a three-cent hammer and a two-cent chisel (stamps inclosed) of a Vesey street fakir, on the way, and don't return without those cupids rampant. I am really in earnest, though this may not sound so. Whitehouse will make trouble if he does not get his umbrella very soon. So please give it attention. Yours faithfully,

HUNTINGTON DUNKLEY.

Two days later I received this reply:

INVENTORS EXPERIMENT COMPANY,

(Paid Up Capital, $50,000,)

INVENTIONS TESTED.   BRIEFS PREPARED.

. J. HIGGINS,
President

. K. RANDALL,
Treas. and Manager.

Bullheimer Building, 217 Broadway,

NEW YORK, _Aug. 28 ___ 189 4

My dear Mr. Dunkley:

Your letter is at hand; and I deeply regret to tell you that Major Whitehouse's family umbrella is not in my possession. —

On reaching Denver I found a telegram awaiting me, from my partner, to look up some mining litigation in Utah, and I started immediately.

That umbrella of course had to be disposed of. — I tried to find you but failed, and so gave it to the first one of our members I met at the station.

The serious part of it is that I can't think which one it was, with any certainty. It is my impression (and a strong impression too) that it was Cobb. — You better write him immediately — Thos. Prolix Cobb, Broadway, Pittsburg, Pa. — I forget the number, just Broadway will do. — As I hadn't heard from you I supposed of course the whole episode was closed —

I am dreadfully sorry & hope the umbrella will turn up all right —

Yours truly — Alfred K. Randall

I live in Elizabeth.

I read Randall's letter through carefully, then I called the office boy, who sits in the outer office, and guards the doors marked "Private."

"William," I said solemnly, "do you know Major D. Pringle Whitehouse when you see him?"

"Yes, sir."

"William, if Major Whitehouse comes in and asks for me, remember that I am now thinking of going to Savannah for a month, and would be gone by the time he gets here. Do you hear?"

William swallowed a couple of times, and said:

"Yes, sir."

"And, William."

"Yes, sir."

"If Major Whitehouse should get in while I am here and actually see me it won't be any use for you to come to work the next morning. That's all."

William retired. I felt safe for the moment, but I knew my device was a weak one. I anathematized the careless and thoughtless Randall, and abused myself for ever relinquishing the umbrella. Upon rereading Randall's letter, my anxiety increased materially. "Couldn't recall which one of our members." We had 3,200 in all, of whom 918 had attended the Denver meeting. Excluding the Major, Randall and myself, there were 915 possibilities. Would it be necessary to circularize all, and even if I did, would that ghostly umbrella ever turn up? I doubted it. The members of the American Association for the Advancement of Invention, were, of course, all honorable men, but the umbrella code of honor seems to have receded before advancing civilization.

I once knew a large, stout man with $10,000 and a scheme. He started an umbrella insurance company. The first month he sent out beautiful lithographed certificates. The second month he sent out checks, and the third month he sent out a notice of assignment. He was a good deal smaller that month in every way, for he had dropped $10,000 and twenty-four pounds of meat.

I began to wonder what I would drop, and concluded I had better write Cobb immediately. That evening I posted this letter:

Thomas P. Cobb, Esq., Broadway, Pittsburg, Penn.

Dear Mr. Cobb: Did you take in the Pike Peak's excursion from the Denver meeting of our association? While up there Major Whitehouse placed a valuable umbrella with an ivory handle (bunch of grapes and cupids rampant) in my hands to bring back to New York. I turned it over to Randall, and he says he gave it to you. If you have it, please send it immediately at my expense to address above. Yours truly,   HUNTINGTON DUNKLEY.

This seemed all I could do for the time being, but the joy had gone out of life. Every time the outer door opened, I stopped work and listened, fearing to hear William's monotonous voice explaining that I was in Savannah. About 2 o'clock I went out for a frugal lunch, which for purposes of safety I took at a humble resort on a side street, but my device was my undoing, for turning a corner on the way back I actually ran into the ample shape and flowing beard of Major D. Pringle Whitehouse.

"Major,"I said with a presence of mind that caused me great self-admiration afterward, "Haven't heard a word about the umbrella yet. Am expecting to hear any day." The Major looked much disappointed.

"I am sorry it has not come," he said. "When had I better call again?"

"Oh, drop in late in the week," I replied, trying to look genial; then pleading business I hurried on, leaving the Major standing in the middle of Nassau street. The thing was really getting serious. So much so that it interfered with my office duties, and even invaded my sleep. That night was the third one to be troubled by dreams of Great Uncle Williams's only bequest.

Two days afterward as I was working at some complicated and exceedingly difficult calculations, I heard a familiar voice in the outer office asking for me.

"Not in, sir," said William.

"Very well, I'll wait."

"No use, sir, he's out of town."

"Is that so, where?"

"Savannah, Georgia, sir."

I shivered.

"Hey?"

"Savannah, sir."

"When'd he go?"

"Tuesday morning, sir."

"Tuesday, hey?"

"Yes, sir; 9 o'clock train, Pennsylvania road. Carried his satchel to the ferry myself, sir. Saw him off."

I shivered again. This time it was a real shiver. I had forgotten to tell William of my accidental meeting with the Major, and here he was dressing up his lie with unnecessary and hideous details. There was a moment's silence in the outer office, and then the Major said:

"Boy, you are lying. I saw Mr. Dunkley Tuesday afternoon on Nassau street myself."

This would never do. It was bad enough to merely state untruthful absence, but while William's street gamin wit would doubtless bring him through, the lie would be colossal and variegated before the Major left. Before he could reply, I flung my door open and looked out.

"Ah, Major," I said cordially, "glad to see

you. I heard William say I had gone to Savannah. I told him I was likely to go, but have been detained. Come in and sit down, Major."

Major Whitehouse cast a wrathful glance at the tranquil William and strode in. His manner lacked its whilom cordiality.

"Any news for me?" he inquired.

"None at all. How does the 'evolution of the trap' progress, Major?"

"Have you heard from Randall?" he inquired, ignoring my feeble effort to change the theme.

"Yes; I had a brief note. He is up in the Catskills, and I presume nothing can be done till he gets back."

"This is exceedingly disappointing to me, Mr. Dunkley," said the Major, with much dignity, looking sharply about my office, as though his Great Uncle's umbrella might appear at any moment from any direction.

"I fully expected some definite word about my umbrella to-day. I trust I have made plain how highly I value it. That umbrella, sir, is thirty-nine years old. It was the only bequest of my Great Uncle Williams to me. He died in 1889. I have carried it constantly since, and I don't propose, sir, to lose it now."

"Major Whitehouse," I said, getting angry at last, "I am heartily sick of this umbrella business."

"So am I, sir," he responded.

"Let me get you a new umbrella."

"I don't want it."

"Silver head."

"I don't want it."

"Gold head."

"I don't want it."

"I'll have an umbrella made for you," I exclaimed, desperately, "with ivory cupids rampant, couchant, passant, from handle to ferrule."

"I don't want it," shouted the Major excitedly.

"I'll give you an umbrella annuity. A new one annually or semi-annually," I urged.

"Mr. Dunkley, you trifle, sir," said the Major, severely. "I am able to buy umbrellas myself. For reasons I have stated I wish my own umbrella, the one I left in your charge. The matter may rest for a week or ten days. When I call again, sir, I expect you to have my umbrella."

Without a goodby or goodday the Major stalked out. I tried to resume work, but that confounded umbrella seemed to pervade and confuse everything I touched. At length I left the office and sought relief at my club. The next three days were made uncomfortable by no tidings from Cobb, but on Monday upon reaching my desk I found an envelope marked Pittsburg, and I opened it with feverish haste. Here is the letter:

THOMAS PORTER COBB,
MINING AND PATENT EXPERT.

Box 42. PITTSBURG, PA. _____ Sept 2 - 189_

Huntington Dudley, Esq.
Philadelphia ——

My dear Sir,

In answer to your letter of the 1st, I
have no knowledge of the relation, finished you after as
left town immediately after the annual meeting of the
American Association for the Advancement of Invention
regretting that business and your absence —

Yours, with great regret

Thomas P. Cobb

P.S. Why not write to Hotchkiss? He was constantly with
Radical and may recall the matter. Maurice P.
Hotchkiss, Northern, Conn., Statin.

I confess to a feeling of intense disappointment. Somehow I had really expected results from Cobb, and it began to look as though a circular to the whole 914 remaining would be necessary. I did write. I wrote immediately.

My Dear Hotchkiss:—

Please tell me whether you brought back from Denver for Randall, or any one else, a big, black silk umbrella, with an ivory handle, carved to represent a bunch of grapes and two cupids rampant. If so, I want it quick. I am in a peck of trouble over this umbrella. While up on Pike's Peak with the association excursion last month Major Whitehouse, of Jersey City, decided to make a hasty trip to California, and, finding his ancestral umbrella would be in the way, he pitched on me to bring it East, and then departed. Of course I could not refuse, but I made some remarks about it later, which Randall heard, and he kindly offered to assume my burden, so I turned the umbrella over to him. Randall was called to Utah on business, and sent the Major's unwelcome property East by some one else. He thought it was T. P. Cobb, of Pittsburg. Cobb thinks it was you. If you have that umbrella for goodness' sake send it. The Major haunts me. Every beard I see gives me a shock. Send the umbrella by express, special delivery, special messenger, but get it here. Yours sincerely,

HUNTINGTON DUNKLEY.

Two more apprehensive days elapsed, and Hotchkiss's reply was before me. It read:

MARCUS P. HOTCHKISS,

GENERAL CONNECTICUT AGENT

THE NEW YORK CHEMICAL CONTRIVANCE CO.,

(ESTABLISHED, 1776.)

New Haven, Conn., Sept. 5th, 1894.

My Dear Dunkley,

I regret to say I cannot send you Whitehouse's umbrella with ivory handle and rampant cupids Perhaps I can aid you however for I was with Randall before he left Denver and I think he turned that Whitehouse relic over to Penfield not A. M. but O. Penfield of Baltimore Don't write him Get a requisition from the Governor and go there yourself It's your only chance with O. Penfield Let me add that it is a special Providence for Whitehouse that I am not the custodian of his nonogenarian 'brell. I have lost three this year and I am looking for an umbrella.

Yours ever.

Marcus P. Hotchkiss.

I laid down the letter and groaned aloud. How long was this to continue? Mechanically I reached for paper and wrote:

Oliver Penfield, Esq., Calvert street, Baltimore, Md.

Dear Mr. Penfield: Have you in your possession a large, black silk umbrella with ivory handle carved to represent two cupids rampant, and a bunch of grapes? If so, it is the one placed in my care by Major Whitehouse, of Jersey City, while we were on the Pike's Peak excursion. He wished me to bring it East for him, and I turned it over to Randall. Randall was called to Utah, and says he gave it to Cobb. Cobb denies all knowledge of it and suggested Hotchkiss. Hotchkiss says he never had it himself, but thinks he remembers it was given in your charge. If so, please send the umbrella to me at your earliest convenience, at my expense, and wire me on receiving this whether you have it. Yours truly,

HUNTINGTON DUNKLEY.

I sealed the letter and mailed it, but the situation was evidently growing worse. Major Whitehouse was staved off by talking of Randall's absence. That would not serve much longer. The Major's visits would be resumed soon, and I could not stand many more of them. Long before the 913 remaining names had been canvassed, I would be lodged in a padded cell somewhere, and labelled "H. Dunkley, violent." The thing was going to my head already. Only the previous afternoon, in ordering some pig iron for our works at Seacaucus, I found myself actually beginning the letter to Great Uncle Williams. If there was only some way to appease the Major, but, alas! there was only one umbrella on earth for the implacable Whitehouse, of Jersey City, and that was Great Uncle Williams's bequest. Doubtless I was the picture of despair as I sat leaning on my desk, when our senior partner came into my office.

"You don't look well, Dunkley," he said, kindly.

"I am not well," I replied.

"Then take a few days off," he exclaimed. "I was just going to speak to you about that Twohig matter in Portland. That's just the thing for you. Go up to Maine yourself, and settle it. The change will do you good."

I thanked him heartily. His suggestion came like a ray of hope. After further consultation I decided to spend a week in Maine, and the next morning found me on the eastbound train. I walked through every car to make sure my evil genius was not on board, and sank into a seat as the train started, with a sense of perfect security and intense relief. The trip was one of the most delightful I have ever known. By contrast with the two previous weeks I was care free. I read, smoked. I watched the landscape, and my fellow-passengers by turns. While lazily observing the stir of arrivals and

departures at Springfield, I noticed that the occupant of the seat directly across the aisle from me
was an exceedingly pretty girl, evidently travelling alone. She was not a new arrival in
the car, for her ticket had been punched and
stuck in the seat in front of her. She was be-
comingly attired in the inevitable shirt waist,
a dark dress of some rough cloth, sailor hat and
red belt. A wealth of light brown hair, becom-
ingly arranged, large brown eyes and an exquisite complexion, made up an ideal picture
of a dainty and independent American girl, for
the whole personality was pervaded by an air
of self-possession and independence. The seat
beside her was occupied by a handsome alligator
skin satchel, and a lunchbox of generous di-
mensions. A parasol or umbrella, I could not
see which, stood in the corner and completed
her travelling equipment. I must confess that
my opposite neighbor was an exceedingly interesting study, and in spite of my efforts to
avoid staring, I found my eyes wandering
across the aisle at frequent intervals. She was
occupied with a magazine, but twice her eyes
met mine, and in a vague agreeable way I felt
that perhaps she was not averse to an occasional
glance from my side of the car, and particularly
so when upon turning quickly around a few
moments later, I discovered she had been in-
specting me critically, a fact which threw both
of us into some confusion.

"Here, Dunkley," I said to myself, "you're too kittenish. An old bachelor making eyes is dreadful," and by way of emphasizing this mental judgment I decided on a trip to the smoker, when something happened that changed the whole situation. A sudden jarring of the car threw my fair neighbor's umbrella to the floor. She regained it, and stood it up directly in my line of vision. I saw that it was not a parasol, but an umbrella and a tall one. Moreover, it had an ivory handle which was strangely familiar. There seemed to be a bunch of grapes and two——I put my hands to my eyes. Good heavens! Was the asylum closing in on me? My horrible error in directing the pig iron order to Uncle Williams flashed across me. Here I was seemingly free at last from that awful umbrella nightmare, and while furtively glancing at a pretty girl in a railway train the first umbrella I see takes on the characteristics of that Whitehouse pest. I looked resolutely out of the window for some minutes, assuring myself that I was a middle-aged idiot. Here was a good-looking girl, who happened to have a handsome umbrella with an ivory handle. Perfectly allowable; anybody with a yearning for ivory-handled umbrellas could gratify it upon consulting a dealer. However, it was natural that I should be sensitive on umbrellas in general and ivory-handled ones in particular.

That was all; nothing serious; why not look again? I did look. The pretty girl was no longer a factor in the case, and as I knew no rule of politeness which forbids staring at an umbrella, I stared steadily. Argue as I would, there was something remarkable about that handle. The design was undoubtedly a bunch of grapes and two figures extraordinarily like cupids. Having decided this point I rested my eyes and meditated.

"Suppose," I thought, "that Great Uncle Williams's umbrella is really across the aisle from me at this moment, with that girl as proprietor. Then all my letters to the 914 members of the American Association for the Advancement of Invention will be in vain, for there is not a woman among them." The conclusion seemed irresistible that it was my immediate duty to inquire about my fair neighbor's umbrella, but I blushed at the mere thought. Yet an hour or so more, perhaps the very next stop, might see that pretty girl and her ivory-handled mystery whisk out of the car, leaving me to continue my idle inquiries of the 914, and to bear the Major's abuse.

The thought was too much. I sprang up quickly, encountering a roguish glance from my pretty neighbor. She would have been provoked to know what a small part she played in my thoughts as I approached her.

"I beg pardon," I said, bowing as politely as I was capable of doing, "your umbrella has such a remarkable handle that I have ventured to ask permission to look at it."

"Certainly," she answered simply, smiling so broadly at my inquiry that I felt surprised.

Lifting her satchel to the floor and drawing her lunchbox closer, she requested me to be seated, and handed me her umbrella with a look of intense amusement. Suddenly the cause of it flashed across me. My query had seemed merely a clumsy device to scrape acquaintance, and so pitifully clumsy as to be convulsively funny. Blushing and horrified, I sank into the seat beside her, and looked at the umbrella with a stony glare, wondering desperately what I could say.

"Are you a connoisseur in umbrellas?" she asked quizzically.

"Well, I—not exactly," I stammered. "I have a friend who has an umbrella."

"Indeed!"

"Yes," I floundered on, not very coherently. "A remarkable umbrella. He inherited it from his Great Uncle Williams. He died in 1889, and left him an only bequest. It's nearly forty years old."

"The bequest is forty years old, or your Great Uncle Williams is?" she asked pityingly.

"Not my great uncle, but my friend's," I exclaimed, horrified to have the Major's nightmare relative loaded upon me.

"And your friend is forty years old?"

"No, his umbrella is."

We both laughed, and it cleared up the situation considerably.

"You see," I exclaimed, getting my senses back by degrees, "my friend's Great Uncle Williams died in 1889, and left him his family umbrella as an only bequest, and it is now nearly forty years old."

"Does he carry it still?"

"Oh, yes; he values it very highly, and it's quite an interesting relic."

I suppose everybody who has been shaken up mentally as I had been makes a break somewhere along the line. My turn was about to come. My fair companion appeared politely interested, and I continued idiotically,

"I've been quite interested in the subject, because lately the old umbrella was lost, and I have tried to help recover it." The real situation was so bluntly apparent to my new acquaintance that her manner changed instantly.

"So you suspect my umbrella of being stolen property?" she asked, coldly.

"Not by any means," I protested.

"I will trouble you for the umbrella, sir," she continued. "Any one is at liberty to admire it, but I cannot permit examination for identification as somebody else's property."

So saying she stood the umbrella up in the corner, and covered the handle with her jacket. The pleasant look of companionship had faded from her face. Evidently my presence was no longer agreeable.

Once more the Major's confounded umbrella had brought me to grief, but I did not propose to yield so easily. Some radical turn was needed, and this time the Major and not I should be sacrificed.

"Please don't condemn me so hastily," I said.

"You have condemned yourself."

"On the contrary, the court isn't open. The judge and clerk went out some time ago for a cheese sandwich."

"When do they return?" she asked with a glimmer of a smile.

"They are just coming in now. You shall be judge and plaintiff, too. Please state your side of the case."

"It is very simple and very conclusive," she said. "You know a man who owned an old umbrella. Lately he lost it. You wanted to help him find it, and seeing a young woman on a railroad train, alone, and with an umbrella remotely resembling the lost one, you accosted her, determined to obtain the umbrella if it appeared at all like your friend's."

She was certainly close to the truth, but I listened with an apparent air of pity.

"Is the court ready for the defence?" I asked.

"It is."

"Then I put in a total denial. The whole umbrella episode is a fiction."

"Your Uncle Williams and all?" she asked in surprise.

"All fiction," I continued calmly. "The fact was I wanted dreadfully to get acquainted with the young lady who sat across the aisle, and I couldn't think how to accomplish it. I racked my brain from Hartford to Springfield for some excuse, and finally cooked up the umbrella episode. I was rather shaky at first, wasn't I?" I inquired.

"Indeed you were," she answered, laughing at the recollection.

"This is the defence," I added, solemnly. "I throw myself on the mercy of the court, and ask for a decision of the case."

My companion was thoroughly mollified.

"The court decides that you are a very wicked man," she said, "and that you told a very large story for a very small reward. For punishment you shall not mention 'umbrella' till we get to Worcester, where I change cars."

I gave a parting glance at her ivory-handled property in the corner. If that umbrella was not the one given me on Pike's Peak it was a well-preserved twin. The size was right; the silk was right; the handle was ivory, carved to represent a bunch of grapes and two cupids rampant. So much I had seen in my hurried and rattled inspection. However, the Major was overboard now, and I had burned my bridges.

"All right," I said, "I would meekly endure a far more terrible punishment than that to earn your society to Worcester."

The hour that followed was a delightful one. We chatted upon all sorts of subjects, and I found that my companion was not only exceedingly pretty, she was also clever. It was evident that she had been carefully educated, and I early learned that she was either a Wellesley student or had graduated from that institution; which, I could not determine, for while she chatted freely on impersonal subjects, she was very wary in referring to herself. My admiration increased rapidly, and I was anxious to obtain some clew to her identity before reaching Worcester, which she had mentioned as her stopping place, and which we were now rapidly approaching. I suggested that we at least exchange names. She laughingly declined, but held up one corner of a dainty cambric handkerchief to my eager gaze, and let me see the word "Mabel." That was all; nothing would induce her to reveal more, and when, at length, I helped her from the car at Worcester, and reluctantly said farewell, beyond her first name and the fact that she stopped at Worcester to merely change for some station in New Hampshire, I had no clew to her identity or home. I watched the dainty, girlish figure with the satchel, lunchbox and the tabooed umbrella, picking her way across the station and longed to follow, which I would gladly have done, if I had not felt sure it would have been considered a liberty. There was little time to debate this, however, for my train was already moving. I swung on board, and returned to my seat with the memory of the farewell smile that my new-found friend had given me as the train started, and a great sense of loneliness and regret. My feelings for the rest of the journey were of the most mixed and unsettled character. The Major and his umbrella were swept out of my mind, and I found that my fair companion had been greatly like a Kansas cyclone. She hadn't lasted long, but she had done great damage.

"As usual, I have been a fool in one act," I said angrily to myself, looking out the window and seeing nothing. "She is the most attractive girl I ever met, and I didn't have tact enough even to learn her name. The world is full of 'Mabels.' That is merely the wisp of straw before the starving donkey. I'm the donkey."

The average man takes pleasure in abusing himself. It is a harmless occupation that relieves pressure and seems to start the mental circulation. After roundly denouncing myself for failing to ascertain the name of my vanished girl friend, and also for not following her, I quieted my feelings by deciding to obtain a Wellesley catalogue at the first opportunity and to investigate every Mabel in the list. I then told myself to calm down.

"You are too old, Dunkley," I said to myself, "to prance around like a college boy. Nature can't stand the strain. Be calm. Descend from the train, old man, as tranquil as you entered it."

The fact remained, however that I had had a delightful adventure and met, even though for a brief hour or two only, a most attractive girl, to whom the adventure was evidently as novel and exciting as it was to me. Added to that was the tantalizing fact that I had either seen and handled Great Uncle Williams's own umbrella, or else one so like it that even the lynx-eyed Whitehouse could not have told them apart. I resigned myself to the inevitable, however, for the adventure was over, and I had no means of continuing it.

On reaching Portland the next morning I went to my hotel and found this telegram, forwarded from New York, awaiting me:

Never had umbrella. Think Ditson, Middletown, Conn., took it. Try him.

O. PENFIELD.

I wrote at once, as follows:

My Dear Professor Ditson:—

I am having a harrowing experience over an umbrella. Have you any property of that sort in your possession that don't belong to you: big black silk affair; ivory handle carved to represent a bunch of grapes and a pair of cupids rampant? If so, I beg of you to ship it to me at once, at my expense. While on the association excursion to Pike's Peak in July Major Whitehouse placed in my charge an umbrella given him by his Great Uncle Williams. It was several centuries old, more or less. I was to bring it East for him, but gave it to Randall. He was called to Utah and says he gave it to Cobb. Cobb denies the charge and says it was given to Hotchkiss. He also sends an emphatic denial, but recalls the umbrella and declares that O. Penfield, of Baltimore, has it. Penfield telegraphed a negative and says to write you. He actually says you have it. I am almost sceptical enough, my dear Professor, to doubt the existence of that umbrella, so if you haven't it don't hesitate to say so, but if you have it, I beg of you to seek the nearest express office at the earliest moment. You little know the terrors of the Major when searching for his own. Yours sincerely,

HUNTINGTON DUNKLEY.

The next three days I occupied attending to business matters, which consumed little time, and enjoying myself, which consumed a great deal of time. I must confess, however, that the fair Mabel had occupied a prominent place in

my thoughts, almost too prominent for a staid
bachelor of thirty-seven, and I began to think
that my trip had added to my woes rather than
lightened them. The fourth day came a letter
from Middletown. It was a large letter with
two stamps on it, which I felt had significance of
some sort, and I opened it hastily. It was as
follows:

September 10, 1894.

My dear Dunkley:-
Your letter arrived during my absence,
which explains delay.   Mr. Randall asked me to
bring the umbrella East for him, and I did so
with pleasure.   I was ignorant, however, of
the previous incident you mention or that it
belonged to Major Whitehouse.   I supposed it
was owned by Mr. Randall, and have awaited some
word from him.   I am mortified to tell you,
however, that I cannot send the umbrella to you
at once.   My daughter Mabel, who has a weakness
for antiques and oddities, took a violent
liking to the old umbrella, and my wife says she
took it with her to New Hampshire last week.
Had I been at home, I should not have permitted
it, but the mischief is done and I can only
apologize.   She will be home October 1st, and
I will send the umbrella to you by express
immediately.
    With much respect, I remain,
            Yours faithfully,

Dawson L. Ditson

P.S. On reading your letter again
it occurs to me that if you leave
Portland before the 1st you may
prefer to obtain the umbrella yourself, as my daughter is in Nashua,
almost on your way. In case
you approve of this, I enclose a
letter of introduction to her.
            D. L. D.

I laid the Professor's letter and its inclosure down. The quest was over, and the Major's elusive umbrella cornered at last; but better than all, the identity of the bewitching Mabel was disclosed. Fate had been hitting me hard for a couple of weeks, but I frankly admitted that handsome reparation was being made now. Few men who long to meet a pretty and unknown girl find a letter of introduction in the morning mail from the girl's own father. I picked up the unsealed envelope and read:

> To Miss Mabel E. Ditson, care Hon. Josiah Eddy, Main street, Nashua, N. H. Introducing Mr. H. Dunkley.

The inclosed note read:

> My Dear Daughter:—
> The umbrella which I brought back from Denver belongs to Major Whitehouse, of Jersey City, and he desires it immediately.
> This will introduce to you Mr. Huntington Dunkley, of New York, a friend of the Major's, and an esteemed friend of mine, to whom please deliver the umbrella at once.
> Mr. Dunkley is the third vice-president of the American Association for the Advancement of Invention, and a young man of high inventive attainments. I commend him most heartily to your favor. Your affectionate father,
> D. L. D.

In three hours my business in Portland was completed, and I was on my way to Nashua. Professor Ditson would have been surprised, I presume, at my haste. He would have been still more surprised, however, at the first chapter of the story.

"There are a good many things the old people don't know," I reflected facetiously. It was wonderful how kittenish I had become. I went over to Nashua that evening from Boston, and readily found the residence of Hon. Josiah Eddy. It was a substantial, old-fashioned New England house, with the usual big white pillars before it. The maid informed me that Miss Ditson was at home, and handing her my card and the letter of introduction, I waited with considerable trepidation in the old-fashioned but well-appointed parlor. There was a brief delay, then a rustle of feminine skirts on the stairs, and my whilom acquaintance of the train stood in the doorway. A look of utter bewilderment came over her face as she recognized the visitor. It almost seemed unfair, for while I understood the situation, her father's note and my card in no way suggested the railway acquaintance to her until she saw me face to face. For a moment she hesitated, blushing, irresolute and almost frightened.

"Please don't treat me like a total stranger, Miss Ditson," I said, rising to meet her, "It has been a great pleasure for me to avail myself of your father's note of introduction. I might better call it a privilege."

Miss Ditson was not a girl to lack self-possession long. She recovered a fair working supply while I spoke, and advancing easily to where I stood, she held out her hand with much cordiality.

"My father's friends are always welcome visitors wherever I am," she said, "but your face is such a familiar one, Mr. Dunkley, that the recognition quite overwhelmed me for a moment."

"It would be hard to twist a compliment out of that," I commented mournfully.

"Don't try," she said, laughingly, "you have enough to do making peace with your conscience."

"What do you mean?"

"You seem to have totally forgotten, sir, your solemn assurances to the court that you had no friend, no Great Uncle Somebody"——

"He wasn't my great uncle," I protested.

"Well, anybody's, then. You denied his existence. Denied even the umbrella. You said it was all for my sake," she pouted, "and it was just a whopper after all. I am glad papa has supplied you with a character, for you need it. Your are a dreadfully wicked, deceitful man."

"You forget the facts, Miss Ditson," I urged. "You misunderstood my explanations in the train, and in consequence were about to dismiss me. Heroic measures were necessary. I threw

my friend and his umbrella completely overboard to preserve your acquaintance. I would
have thrown anything else over to keep it,"
I added fervently. "Was I not justified?"

"Perhaps," she said, with a glance that
thrilled me. "Any way, I mustn't be too severe,
for I am far from blameless myself. Indeed,
your opinion of me must be dreadful. Now,
Mr. Dunkley," she went on giving me no chance
to protest, "you must lay the umbrella subject
aside for this evening, anyway."

"Certainly," I said, "I did not call to discuss
umbrellas."

"I thought that was your favorite theme?"

"It isn't. I can talk about anything. Try
me."

"I will," she answered, laughing, "but I wish
to introduce you to my uncle and his family,
and then I am going to take you with me to a
little informal party nearby."

"I am not dressed for it," I protested.

"Yes, you are."

"Very well, I am a willing victim," I said,
though inwardly regretting that I could not
have Miss Mabel all to myself.

I spent that night as Mr. Eddy's guest, for
he would not hear of my return to Boston after
the pleasant evening passed with his family,
and a hotel, he declared, was inhospitable. The
next day there was to be a drive to Milford for

autumn leaves, and I had been promptly included. Although the party was a pleasant one, I had eyes for Miss Mabel only, and as she was gracious, the day was a delightful one to me. That evening I returned to Boston, but before leaving I had solemnly promised to come back the next day for a week, to participate in several festivities. The days that followed were blissful ones for me. What Mabel's thoughts were I knew not. My own were clear. I was head over heels in love with the pretty, coquettish girl, and it was enough to be with her and near her. We made excursions together into the surrounding country, now doubly beautiful with the first touches of autumn.

There are some parts of our land where summer seems to dry up and blow away, but in New England her passing is in garments of radiant beauty. First a faint blush on all the landscape, growing deeper, until, seemingly at once, the whole horizon is ablaze with endless, wondrous harmonies of color, on hill and forest; the dull brown-green of August has yielded to tints no flowers can ever equal, no canvas reproduce.

I did not look too closely into the future, content to let it bring its own problems, but meantime I spared no effort and no expense to make myself agreeable and to win Miss Ditson's favor. The Major and his umbrella had almost faded from my thoughts. True, she had not given me the umbrella, but it was here, and safe, and that was enough. The Major, bad luck to him, must wait. I was attending to my own business now. Once or twice I had referred to Great Uncle Williams's ancestral property, but Miss Mabel had laughingly turned the subject to something else. I had noticed, moreover, that she now used a dainty and modern blue silk umbrella, which I took to be a delicate acknowledgment of relinquished ownership in the big one.

In rides, excursions and parties the week passed delightfully. By general request I lengthened my visit another two days to participate in a final excursion to the shore. The intervening day Miss Mabel and I proposed to occupy by walking out into the country for chestnuts. Before we started the morning mail brought me a letter in a scrawling hand. I opened it with some curiosity and read:

The Brunswick,
Jersey City Heights.

September 20th

H. Dunkley, Sir

Yesterday I went to
Brick Church to investigate the
statements you made about
Randall's house. The P.O. and Express people knew nothing of him.
I went over to Orange and
consulted the Directory of that
town, and walked 3 miles out
on the Valley Road to find that
the only A.R. was a negro.
I do not propose, Sir, to
trifle with you any longer about
my umbrella. This talk about
Randall I consider nonsense
and unless you return my umbrella
within five days I shall begin
legal proceedings. D. Pringle Whitehouse

I put the letter in my pocket. It was the first jarring note of the week. An hour later Miss Mabel and I were strolling toward the outskirts of the city

"I'm afraid, Miss Ditson," I remarked, recalling the letter in my pocket, "that we must box up your adopted umbrella to-night and ship it to the Major. He is getting excited."

Miss Mabel did not answer. I glanced at her and noticed that the color had left her cheeks.

"Would you rather wait till you return to Middletown?" I inquired.

"I may as well tell you the truth at once, Mr. Dunkley," she said in low tones, "the umbrella is not in my possession."

"Then where is it," I asked in astonishment.

"I do not know." Tears of mortification and embarrassment came to her eyes. "It is lost," she faltered. "When I left the train which I took after leaving you at Worcester I must have forgotten it, and permitted it to remain in the seat, for after reaching my uncle's house I was horrified to discover that the umbrella was missing. I went to the station immediately and offered a reward. I telegraphed the general office in Boston. It has done no good. The umbrella is lost, and I cannot tell you what my feelings have been. I knew this moment must come, but oh how I have dreaded it, and

hoping my efforts might produce some result
I have kept you here, and tried to prevent you
from thinking of the subject. Oh, Mr. Dunkley," she added, impetuously, "what a wretched
girl you must think me. Can you ever forgive
such carelessness and duplicity?"

"There is nothing to forgive, Miss Mabel," I
said, sadly. "The umbrella is absolutely nothing to me. Something else grieves me far more.
Yes, overwhelms me."

"What is it?" she asked apprehensively.

"I have been telling myself day after day that
your cordiality and favor showed that I was
not distasteful to you, and from that I dared to
hope for even more. You have shattered all my
dearest hopes by telling me your favor to me
was a matter of calculation to stave off ad-
mitting the loss of an umbrella."

"Oh, not at all—not so bad as that," she protested, eagerly.

"And that my visit and my entertainment
were prompted and designed to prolong concealment," I added bitterly.

My companion made no reply. She seemed
overwhelmed.

"While I regret the loss of the umbrella, it
does not merit a second thought, but I feel
angry and hurt at the feigned esteem for myself."

Something I had said stung Miss Mabel to
momentary anger.

"Oh, don't let that trouble you," she said coldly. "I like you. I couldn't help it. You know papa wrote you I had a weakness for antiques and oddities."

This was a shot I was not prepared for, and I was about to retort sharply, when I noticed that my companion had collapsed agan, and that the tears were trickling down her cheeks. My anger was gone in a second.

"It's all the Major's umbrella," I said to myself. "It has made me miserable for a month, and now the wretched thing has cast its blight on her life. Here and now I end the Major."

"Miss Mabel," I said, gently, stopping in our walk and facing her. "We are having some explanations this morning that may in the end do us both good. Set your mind at rest about the umbrella. I am thankful it is gone. May it never return."

"I thought it was terribly valuable," she said in surprise.

"There is something else of far greater value and importance to me," I continued eagerly, "for it involves the happiness of a lifetime. The idle quest for an old umbrella was long ago swallowed up and lost in the quest for your friendship and—love."

My companion started and walked on. "We shall never find chestnuts at this rate, Mr.

Dunkley," she said, looking back at me with a suggestion of returning pertness.

"I cannot trifle now, Miss Mabel. In a few hours I shall start for Boston. Let us have a plain understanding before I go. Whatever you think of me, remember now, and when I have left you, that the devotion and love of my life have been laid at your feet. Is there no chance of my winning your love in return?"

Silence.

"Miss Mabel," I went on impetuously, "do you remember the court that we held that day on the train?"

"When the judge and the clerk went out for a cheese sandwich?" she asked, smiling faintly.

"Yes. You were the judge and the plaintiff then. Now the court is in session again. This time you are judge alone. You have heard the plea. Do not send me away! My happiness —Oh, Mabel, my all, depends upon your decision."

I tried to control myself, but my voice faltered with intensity of feeling as I paused.

We had stopped again in our walk. The spot was a secluded one on the outskirts of the city, and though there were houses near, they stood at increasing intervals. Back of us was a high fence, over which extended the brilliantly clad branches of a large maple, the fallen leaves of which formed a yellow carpet beneath us. Ma-

bel was still silent. She pushed a dead leaf
along with the toe of her dainty little shoe,
and then with a glance far more eloquent than
words, she said:

"The court decides in the affirmative, with
costs."

I didn't wait for more. I took that dear girl
in my arms and kissed her with a fervor that
spoke the devotion of a lifetime. I suppose it
was seen. I don't care if it was.

"What are the costs, Mabel?' I asked.

"You paid them just now," she replied, blush-
ingly.

A Common Sense Cupid.

The thronging noises of the great city, sub-
dued by midnight, but never ceasing, came
distantly over the housetops to the windows
of the tall bachelor apartment-house where
Arthur Hanford occupied a modest parlor and
bedroom, but they did not serve to distract
him from his own engrossing thoughts, which,
beginning apparently with an open letter on the
table, had carried him many years and many
miles away.

Stroke by stroke, each more delayed and doubt-
ful than the last, the little French clock on
the mantel struck 12, midnight. Hanford's
clock always had especial difficulty with midnight, and on this particular occasion seemed
to give an asthmatic gasp of relief that the
twelve strokes had been duly accomplished
without mishap—which, of course, was entirely
from the standpoint of the little French clock

—not Hanford's, for Hanford was acting strangely. A busy, active man of affairs, he was not ordinarily given to fits of abstraction, yet on this particular evening he had been sitting in his easy chair for two hours, completely lost in thought that was evidently saddening in the extreme.

Arthur Hanford was a tall, well-built man, with brown hair and mustache, the former touched here and there with a gray line or two, more indicative of hard work than age, for he was still a "young man," when that hard-worked phrase was made courteously broad in its application.

Now that the little French clock had served notice of midnight in vain, the outlook for its owner's speedy mental return to everyday matters was discouraging, and it had settled down to a steady all-night tick, when the door was opened without the suspicion of a knock, and a plain-featured young man of perhaps thirty years, entered. "I saw your light, Hanford," he remarked, making himself comfortable on the sofa, "so I ventured to drop in. Can't sleep so early myself. After a year on a night desk in a newspaper office, you might as well chase a rainbow as a snore, before 1 o'clock."

"Then you are back on day work, are you, Watson," said Hanford, apparently not surprised at his visitor's arrival.

"Sorry to say I am, and in consequence my nights, from 8 to 1, are mere vacant spaces—ten-acre lots of time, so to speak, a portion of which I am now prepared to devote to you—unless you are busy," he added.

"No, I am not busy," replied Hanford, quietly. "I received a letter this evening," he continued, "that has affected me considerably, and I have wasted hours in profitless thoughts."

"Thoughts," rejoined Watson, sententiously, "are poor companions after the age of thirty, for the 'might have beens' begin to appear, and make things uncomfortable. Before thirty it is all 'may be,' which, of course, is all right. In your case, Hanford, you are beyond the thirty line. You have no business to think."

"I fear you are right," said Hanford, wearily. "This letter has brought old times back to me thick and fast."

"Meditation in its most aggravated form—from a letter," remarked Watson.

"Why so?"

"Well, a letter generally indicates a woman in the case. Am I right?"

"You are."

"And a woman in the case indicates that the 'might have been' microbes are simply countless. Am I right?"

"You are."

There was something in Hanford's saddened

and lifeless manner that attracted his friend's attention. They were opposites in temperament and appearance, thrown much together; first, because they lived across the hall from each other, and afterward because a genuine affection had sprung up between them.

Watson was a man of few natural advantages. Plain-looking and one of those unfortunate men upon whom everything seemed ill-proportioned, his features were irregular, and his thin and refractory beard was thickest where least desired. A sensitive appreciation of his own physical defects made him extremely diffident with the other sex, and his conversation often took the careless and cynical tone which frequently occurs when a man's associates are almost entirely masculine. Yet beneath a rough and somewhat careless exterior, there were depths of unstirred tenderness and unselfish devotion. The existence of these qualities, though unnoticed and perhaps by some unsuspected, served nevertheless to make him a trusted friend, and Hanford's apartment was not the only one in the big building where Watson's rough personality and crisp and original remarks were always welcome.

"It has long been a belief of mine," he said, watching his friend closely, and wondering how he could aid him, "that most of the 'might have beens' are totally inexcusable. We human beings have the unhappy faculty of blundering at a crisis. The head should be clearest at the most critical moment. As a matter of fact, it seldom or never is."

"Possibly you are right," said Hanford, "but I am fatalist enough to doubt it."

"You should not."

"Why?"

"Because it is generally a question of common-sense. Most of us possess that inestimable gift, but too often we ignore it."

"Common-sense does not apply to affairs of the heart," said Hanford.

"So lovers always declare. I never understood why. Perhaps I shall when the tender passion smites me. They take your standpoint; smile a sad smile; say, 'Oh, no,' and suffer. I take it your present trouble is a love affair of some sort, and I'll wager most anything that there is a lack of common-sense tied up in it somewhere."

"I don't believe in a common-sense Cupid," said Hanford, shortly.

"Come, Hanford, what is the trouble? If it isn't indelicate to ask it, may I hear the story? My theories may be wrong, but I should like to test them." Watson's tone was hearty and sympathetic. He looked anxiously at his friend, feeling sure from his voice and manner that some serious trouble had overtaken him.

"I don't mind telling you about it, Watson. Indeed, it may do me good to talk to a trusted friend, but it will probably bore you. There is nothing thrilling or dramatic in the story."

"Glad to hear it," interposed Watson. "We keep that sort of thing for Sunday specials. This is a week day. Go ahead, but first lend me a pipe. Without tobacco, conversation after midnight, as Shakespeare sweetly observes, 'is a wasteful and ridiculous excess.'" Saying which he filled and lighted a cob pipe from his friend's tray, and resumed his comfortable attitude on the sofa. "To apply my common-sense method which you object to," he continued, "to affairs of sentiment, we ought, of course, to have the facts. I should not feel competent to advise you in a love affair actually in progress, nor, indeed, should I be justified in intruding argument and platitude under those circumstances. That would be simply a case of vivisection. I take it this case is old enough to permit discussion without indelicacy."

"Old enough, yes." Hanford paused. His thoughts seemed again to have strayed from his little parlor and his friend's companionship.

"The incident was one of my youth," he said after a moment's silence. "To the girl it is an old and long-forgotten story. To me—well, you needn't mind me. Here it is:

"You have often heard me refer to my college

life and the mistake I made, considering my present occupation, of fitting myself at a technical school to be a mining engineer. I think, however, that I have seldom mentioned the two years which followed graduation. Indeed, to look back on them, they seem like a dream to me. They represented an earnest attempt to follow my chosen profession, and were years of great effort and unrequited labor.

"On concluding my course at college, I advertised in the technical papers for employment and received one reply. It came from a man in Boston, who said he desired some special work performed in the way of mineralogical research, and suggested an interview. I went to Boston and found my inquirer represented a syndicate prepared to search for iron ore.

"Perhaps you know that the western, or New York, shore of Lake Champlain is rich in iron deposits, which are profitably mined at several points. The whole western shore is wild and rugged, while the Vermont shore opposite is level, accessible and highly cultivated.

"The syndicate believed that a careful investigation would disclose iron ore at some point along the Vermont shore, of better quality and more easily mined. If ore could be found containing magnetic qualities it would be of immense value.

"After some negotiation, I was engaged for

my expenses and a trifling salary besides, to make a thorough examination of the eastern shore, my incentive to diligence and success lying in a handsome bonus offered by my employers for the desired discovery.

"I began immediately, and deciding that my outside work must be done during the summer months, I settled on a small village just below Burlington as my headquarters, and obtained lodgings. There I remained for several weeks, making a careful study of the geological formation of that region, and then set out on a mile-by-mile observation of the shore, making a chart and obtaining specimens of rock formation.

"Once a week I returned to my headquarters and labelled and arranged my specimens for future study.

"I need not tell you that my waking hours were not all devoted to the search for ore, though I labored long and faithfully to that end. The village I had chosen for my temporary home was beautifully located, perhaps half a mile from the lake, though from that side only the white spire was visible. It was a farming village, like most Vermont towns, peaceful and spotless, with its common, its white houses and elms, and that air of substantial comfor' so characteristic of New England, and so seldom seen elsewhere.

"The village itself was a mere hamlet. There were three stores and perhaps fifty houses altogether. I early learned, however, that there was one leading and dominating spirit in the community.

"Vermont elects a Governor annually, and, in consequence, her ex-Governors are innumerable. One of them, ex-Governor Milbank, lived in the village and he controlled it mentally, socially and financially.

"The Governor was a man of large property, and though living in a rural community, was far from being provincial. His house, the most pretentious in town, was surrounded by lawns and shrubbery, and was furnished in perfect taste. It was a gentleman's house in every particular, and as both the Governor and his family travelled much, they had accumulated many objects of interest from other lands.

"When I went to Lyndon, Governor Milbank was a well-preserved man of sixty. His wife was a cultivated and agreeable woman. Their large family, consisting of four sons and four daughters, was much scattered. Three sons had married and settled down at distant points; two daughters were also married; and of the two at home unmarried, cne was not over sixteen, still a schoolgirl."

Hanford paused, while his friend refilled the cob pipe.

"Eligible young men, as you doubtless know," he resumed, "do not teem in country villages, and my arrival was soon known in the Governor's house. I sought an introduction, and before long I became a welcome visitor, dropping in frequently whenever I reached town from one of my numerous expeditions. Somehow I found the younger daughter the most companionable member of the family. Her elder sister was older than I and a fine girl, but much occupied with the affairs of the household or the many and ramifying interests outside.

"The young son at home was a shy, retiring boy, with whom I had little in common. After my trips I generally took a day off, and if I needed a companion for a walk, a fishing excursion to the nearby shore, an opponent at tennis or, in short, a congenial associate, Kathleen Milbank was always ready.

"She would not have been called pretty, but she had a vivacious, attractive face, graceful figure and manners that were unaffected and indescribably pleasing. She was the most companionable girl I ever met, an inveterate flirt, as romantic as her age suggested, bubbling over with animal spirits and good nature. She showed the influence of careful rearing, for she had a large store of good sense, and in her quieter moods gave glimpses of the genuine, earnest womanhood to come.

"Kathleen was eight years younger than I, which means more at that age than it does later, and while I regarded her as an ideal companion I studiously avoided anything sentimental, in spite of the opportunity which her age and romantic disposition offered. It never occurred to me to analyze this. It came, I suppose, from a feeling that trifling might lead to serious results, and as I was older and more experienced I had no right to take such a course.

"We had both had affairs of the heart, at least we called them so, and Kathleen related hers with deepest interest and laughing eyes, especially her school escapades.

"A favorite resort of ours was a bluff on the lake shore, about a mile to the southward, where a tongue of land jutted into the lake, breaking the uniform shore line and forming a bay. On this bluff Burgoyne had encamped for a day or two during his ill-fated expedition to Saratoga, and had left a permanent reminder of himself in rude earthworks, still dimly visible. Here beneath a sentinel elm we spent many pleasant hours reading and talking.

"Kathleen had ideas of her own, which she expressed remarkably well. She acted as an intellectual stimulant to me, and our discussions on all sorts of topics were of value to us both.

"Gradually my association with Miss Kathleen became the most delightful feature of my life at the lake, and I found myself looking forward to our weekly excursions with considerable interest. Do not imagine, however, that I neglected the rest of the family, for I found them all agreeable friends, and felt in return that I was liked by them.

"There were occasional visitors, young people of both sexes, at the Governor's house, and at such times I shortened my stay in the village and made my excursions especially lengthy and thorough.

" 'She doesn't want me around,' I reasoned. 'I am welcome when younger and more congenial companions are lacking, but when they are present I ought to be absent.'

"This policy I regarded at the time as a lofty exhibition of disinterested friendship. Perhaps at this distance I can see a different reason, unsuspected at the time.

"In September Kathleen left for boarding school, and in spite of my independence and the positive assurances I gave myself, the town lost interest for me immediately. As my season was practically over, I packed up my data and samples, and early in October departed for Boston, having completed about two-thirds of my task. The winter was occupied in working out my notes and testing specimens. Several of the latter showed encouraging results, and my employers were so well pleased that they decided to have me complete my work the following season. Accordingly, when the spring was well advanced, I resumed my old quarters and mode of life.

"Kathleen and I had exchanged letters occasionally during the winter, and I had seen her twice, so the gap made by the separation was not especially wide. We fell back into our old ways, companionship and excursions, in the most natural and comfortable style, and the summer sped away in this congenial combination of work and holiday.

" 'I do not care for Kathleen except as a jolly girl friend,' I kept saying to myself, 'and she cares nothing for me except in the same way. There are two or three young sprigs who stand far higher with her sentimentally than I do, and I am glad of it, for, of course, I am much older, and I am not laying siege to her heart, so sentiment must be kept out.' I did not notice that the very vehemence of this argument with myself indicated something amiss.

"Thus the last weeks of my stay passed, and as they approached a close I was conscious that an indefinable dread was settling over me, which, in spite of every effort, I could not shake off.

"At length, one afternoon in late August, as we sat under the elms on the bluff, I was about to tell her of my completed work and speedy departure. I had been giving her a lesson in sketching, and she suddenly looked up and said:

" 'You are a great comfort, Mr. Hanford.'

" 'Thanks,' I replied, 'I'm like tea—cheer but don't inebriate.'

" 'You have turned two dull summers into pleasant and profitable ones,' she continued, 'and by the end of the season your pupil in literature and drawing will demand a diploma from the Hanford Summer School.'

" 'The Hanford Summer School, as you call it, Miss Kathleen,' I answered quietly, 'will close its sessions to-day for good.'

" 'What do you mean?' she demanded, with the slightest perceptible start.

" 'Merely that my work is complete. I think that I have found what I came for, and I must go back to Boston as quickly as I can, to work up my data. I have postponed telling you because—well, I couldn't bear to do it, that's all.'

"The sun was sinking in a gorgeous bank of clouds across the lake. Kathleen put away her sketching materials. She was very quiet.

" 'We shall say goodby to-night, Miss Kathleen,' I continued, as we started homeward, 'in public, at your house, but while we are alone I want to tell you that I count the hours we have spent together as the most delightful I have . known. I realize that I have failed, perhaps through temperament and age, to be of—of absorbing interest to you, but that doesn't alter my sentiments or my enjoyment of the society of one of the loveliest and most accomplished girls in Vermont.'

" 'The Flattery Course in the Hanford Summer School is short but violent,' said Kathleen. 'Omit the compliments, please, Mr. Hanford. We have passed some delightful hours together for two summers. You have played the role of Old Man to your own satisfaction, and now that the curtain is rung down we will part good friends. Is there any probability that the Young Girl in Vermont will ever again see the Old Man from Boston?' Her tone had become light and careless.

" 'If his affairs prosper, yes,' I replied. A feeling of intense disappointment and bitterness came over me as I answered, and there was silence for some minutes as we walked beside each other.

"Somehow a sudden coolness, unknown before, unexpected now, had sprung up between us. With it came the sudden realization that I loved the girl beside me, and with an intensity before undreamed of.

"A moment later we reached the west gate of the Milbank lawn.

" 'Kathleen,' I said, impetuously, taking the hand she held out as she turned to complete her careless farewell, 'whatever you think of me, don't let us part like this. I have been the pastime of a summer day for you. It has been more than that to me—more than I have dared to think or say, and now that the day is over, we part, and apparently you have not even enough interest to be kind,' I added bitterly.

"I felt her hand tremble in my grasp. She drew it away as I paused, and before I guessed her purpose, unpinned a bit of goldenrod which she had worn on our excursion, laid it, silver pin and all, in my hand, and with one blushing, radiant glance, was gone."

Hanford stopped his narrative and walked to the window. He seemed overcome by the thronging memories which his story recalled.

"Well?" said Watson interrogatively, at length.

"There isn't any 'well' about it," rejoined Hanford irritably. "That's all."

"All?"

"Yes. I called that evening to bid the family goodby, and Miss Kathleen was invisible. She sent a cordial farewell by her mother.

"The next morning I left for Boston, where I learned that while my researches had been partially successful, the syndicate had not.

"Their disagreements were brought to a head by the failure and death of the principal promoter of the plan; the whole scheme fell through, and I found myself with considerable arrears of salary and expenses, completely without redress, nor was I ever able afterward to collect a cent, for the contract proved defective.

"Thus handicapped and deeply discouraged, I came to New York, abandoned my profession, and took the first employment that offered. It brought me neither honor nor money; merely existence. My pride prevented explanations to Kathleen. Of course, I was not able to visit her, and though I wrote her at intervals, our letters were not satisfactory. The years that followed were years of sharp conflict for me—years of unremitting toil and much privation. I became engrossed in my business ventures, and only within the last three months have I begun to see myself master of my own affairs. I had struggled and saved, educated my two sisters and won independence for myself. At length I could do justice to my own yearnings, which were ever toward Kathleen, but to-night, returning to my apartment, I found an invitation to her wedding."

Hanford paused a moment to recover his composure.

"That's all, Watson," he concluded. "I didn't mean to inflict it on you at such length, but somehow it told itself. All but my own feelings. A man who sees the hopes, plans and dreams of his life suddenly swept out of existence can't describe them as they go.

"Now, you can moralize, old fellow. There may be some vivisection, as you call it, but never mind, go ahead, for two weeks from to-morrow," he added bitterly, "Kathleen Milbank will be some one else's wife."

Watson made no immediate reply. His friend walked up and down the room in gloomy silence, the prey to a swarm of unhappy thoughts.

"Hanford, do you want to know what I think of you?" asked Watson, at length.

"I suppose so."

"You are about as big a fool as I ever met."

"Why?" asked his friend humbly.

"Because the wreck of your happiness is entirely your own fault. You won the love of a sweet girl, said nothing more, and left her. Then you plunged into business with varying success. You forgot that she had time for thought. Underneath, you cherished a genuine affection, which you proposed to bring out properly caparisoned, when you were ready, and somehow expected to find the girl waiting. Instead, you are surprised to learn that she belongs to another."

"It's an old story, I suppose," said Hanford gloomily.

"Perhaps it is, but it wouldn't be such an old story if people used a little common-sense, as I said when we began."

"Hang your common-sense," exclaimed Hanford irritably. "It's easy for a man without a love affair to moralize to a man who has one. The whole realm of sentiment is built on the opposite idea. A common-sense Cupid couldn't exist."

"A common-sense statement of your case is this," continued Watson, ignoring the interruption. "You loved a girl, and you had reason to believe she loved you, but your affairs would not permit you to marry her speedily. Common-sense and common justice demanded that you have a plain talk with her, and if she loved you and was any kind of a girl, she would stick to you for years, waiting till you were able to marry her."

"It would have been unjust to Kathleen to pin her down to an uncertain future like mine," urged Hanford.

"Not if she loved you. That isn't a woman's way of arguing. Time enough to release her when you had tried and failed. Your failure to be sensible has worked injustice to you both. Talk of your feelings, Hanford; what have hers been during these years while faith in you turned slowly to doubt and anxiety, and that to bitterness and indifference?"

Hanford winced.

"These are the might have beens," continued Watson, noting his advantage. "Merely the common-sense Cupid you jeer at, applied to the past; now what of the future?" Watson arose.

"Arthur Hanford," he said with an earnestness that his friend had never before seen him exhibit, "I said at the outset that I wouldn't pretend to advise a man on a current love affair. I do pretend to advise you now, for there is a high and manly duty before you. Mark this well. One of two conditions exists at this moment. Either Miss Kathleen, disgusted by years of neglect and waiting, has forgotten you completely and turned to others, or else she still cares for you, but has become discouraged by your neglect and yielded to the importunities of another. You've treated the girl shamefully, and now you have reached a crisis in her life and yours. It's your duty to see her and to see her now. Tell her all—your trials, privations and faith.

"If she is immovable, and annoyed at your advances, you've proved to your own satisfaction that her love for you is at length completely dead, and whatever your own feelings, you will at least be absolved from the responsibility of having destroyed her happiness by your conduct. On the other hand, if by any possibility she should still cherish your image in her heart, you can save her from a life of sorrow and win your own happiness besides."

"The cards are already out, Watson," faltered Hanford, deeply agitated.

"That means hours and days to spare," retorted Watson, with an intensity that fired his friend. "I am a plain, blunt man, Arthur Hanford, but I see a duty when it lies before me as plainly as yours, and in this case it is partially a question of honorable dealing. There is only one course to pursue. I could hardly respect you or even speak to you if you didn't follow it. That isn't a threat, old fellow," he added in a gentler tone, throwing his arm upon his friend's shoulder in the half-caress which a man sometimes uses to another. "I know you too well, Hanford, to doubt you. You are a strong-willed, true-hearted man. The very record of your devotion to Miss Milbank proves it. There is your duty; you will follow it, and just suppose—mind, I don't think it probable, but then—goodby, and good luck."

For an hour by the little French clock Arthur Hanford struggled with his own despondency, but when Watson arose in the morning he found a card beneath the door and on it was penciled:

"Dear Watson: Have taken morning train. Will telegraph you. A. H."

II.

Hanford had ample time for reflection during the long hours of that Tuesday in late September as the train rolled northward.

He was not averse to reflection. There have

been a few master minds of lightning action. Doubtless some still exist capable of grasping a complex situation without reflection and adapting themselves to any emergency, but most of us prefer an opportunity to withdraw the scattered forces of the brain from the field of battle, and to reorganize their broken ranks in preparation for new conflicts.

Hanford had fallen into a method of thought regarding his affairs of sentiment which was now sadly shattered. He had trained himself for years to a policy of repression. Accompanying this had grown up the vague belief that when his own wishes could be considered and he could make them known, everything would come out satisfactorily.

The violence of the shock attested how far this idea had become rooted in his mind.

His friend's aggressive advice, and his unwonted earnestness in urging it, had added another host of considerations, and now for the first time, with the rush of the train and the knowledge that action of some sort lay before, came comparative tranquillity and the opportunity to set his mind in order for the new conflict.

Doubtless Hanford's thoughts were not all of the common-sense order. Perhaps even Watson would not have expected that. Certainly the contending emotions which arise from such an experience greatly influence thought and conduct, and make it difficult to follow a logical course.

Out of the throng of thoughts which crowded upon him came the increasing conviction that however conscientious and self-sacrificing he had been, his policy had been a fatally erroneous one. This brought the twin conviction that his friend's advice was sound. and that he was now following a plain duty.

Intent, however, upon avoiding another blow such as he had received, Hanford assured himself again and again that he had not the slightest hope of his own success. Things had gone too far for that. His journey was solely to justify his own conduct and assure himself of Kathleen's happiness.

The mind, however, is a headstrong servant. We do not always realize the hopes it cherishes until their destruction brings us pain.

Having decided the question of his past conduct against himself, and approved with increasing heartiness of the trip he had undertaken, Hanford set himself to outlining a plan of campaign. Wearied at length with the innumerable possibilities liable to arise and overthrow any set scheme, he arranged a simple programme to produce opportunity, and determined to let everything else arise spontaneously from his sense of honor, manliness and affection.

The trip at length drew to a close, and in the twilight of the shortening fall day Lyndon was reached. In the early morning, before leaving the city, Hanford had visited a fashionable florist on Broadway and secured a box of the finest orchids obtainable upon such a hasty order and had had them packed with extreme care. This box, which he had jealously guarded throughout the trip from officious porters, he addressed to Miss Kathleen Milbank, and as the train stopped he intercepted the station agent as that worthy was about to attack the baggage-car and said:

"Can you deliver a package for me this evening with absolute certainty if I pay you enough twice over?"

"I guess there ain't much doubt about it," answered the surprised agent, forgetting the baggage-car for the moment.

"Here's the money," said Hanford, passing a liberal fee into the agent's hand. "Deliver this box to Miss Milbank this evening—at the earliest moment you can after this train leaves. Can I depend on you?"

"You can. I'll give it to her myself."

Hanford's first move was made. He returned to the train and went on to Burlington, where he sought a hotel and much-needed repose.

Early that evening Miss Kathleen Milbank examined with surprise and delight the exquisite contents of Hanford's box. Within it she found this note:

"My Dear Miss Kathleen. The invitation to your wedding has reached me just as I am starting for Montreal on business.

"Permit me to offer these flowers as an advance-guard of innumerable good wishes which I am anxious to express in person. I know how occupied you must be, but may I have an hour with you to-morrow afternoon, for an oldtime walk and chat?

"I shall be in Burlington all the morning, and a dispatch will reach me at the Van Ness.

"Faithfully,   ARTHUR HANFORD."

Emerging from breakfast the next morning a telegram was handed to him. It read:

"Shall be delighted to see you as proposed at 3 o'clock.   K. M."

The early afternoon found Hanford strolling up the familiar shaded walk to the Governor's house, outwardly calm, but keenly realizing how much depended on the events of that afternoon. A gentle breeze moved in the treetops, and the soft haze of September hung over the landscape. A moment more and he found himself in the well-remembered parlors, heard a light step on the stair, and Kathleen Milbank stood before him with the cordial, unaffected greeting of an old friend.

To Hanford's eager glance she had changed little. The years had brought maturity to face and figure, which more than bore out the pleasing promise of her youth. Her large blue eyes beneath delicately arched brows still looked as

frankly forth upon the world as they did in
girlhood, and the singular charm of voice and
manner, which had made her a favorite in the
village from her earliest years, was still apparent, though softened by an indefinable dignity and maturity. She wore a pink dress of
some soft summer material, and a large white
hat trimmed with pink roses. So hearty and un-
embarrassed was Kathleen's greeting as Hanford stepped forward and took her hand that he
vaguely wondered whether it would not have
been better strategy to have surprised her and
thus have been able perhaps to gather some
clew to her feelings from her deportment. "It
is all useless, though," he thought, bitterly. "I
have sunk to the low level of a casual acquaintance, and must be careful lest my call outlives
my welcome."

"That exquisite box which reached me last
evening, Mr. Hanford," said Kathleen, "was a
delightful surprise, not only in the contents, but
in the prospect it brought for to-day, and you
see I have my hat on already in anticipation.
Our old haunts are all the same, except May-
nard's wharf, which caved in three winters
ago."

"How about the bluff?" asked Hanford. "Is
there a summer hotel there yet?"

"Your inquiry is a year early," replied Kathleen, laughing; "the bluff has been sold, and

there is to be a big hotel erected there next spring."

"I hope they haven't begun work yet," interposed Hanford, anxiously, "for I confess to a weakness for the bluff. Is it still the same?"

"I believe so," said Kathleen. "I seldom or never go there."

In a vague, indefinite way Hanford felt pleased.

"Suppose we walk in that direction, anyway," he suggested.

"Gladly," she answered, arising; "but you must first let my mother and sister welcome you, and promise to remain to supper with us."

A few moments later they were strolling along the well-remembered path to the lake. Hanford was conscious that he himself had improved in the years which had elapsed since their parting. Success is a great factor in any one's deportment. Under it a small-minded man grows pompous, but to a man of cultured sensibilities success brings the confidence required to complete good manners. Hanford belonged to the latter class. His deportment, always that of a gentleman, had measurably improved in ease and grace.

There was much to talk about, even had they avoided reminiscences. Hanford answered Kathleen's kindly inquiries about himself courteously but briefly—that subject would come up later.

"I wrote you, Miss Kathleen," he said, "that I wanted to deliver my congratulations to you in person, and now that I try to do so, your welfare is so dear to me that I hardly know how to express with sufficient earnestness my hope for its continuance and your life-long happiness."

"I appreciate what you say, Mr. Hanford," said Kathleen, quietly. "I expect to be very happy. Colonel Ware is a noble, generous-hearted man. He is much older than I, but his devotion is unwavering, and I am proud to have won his affection. Unfortunately he is an Englishman, and lives in Toronto, which greatly grieves my father, but one cannot control matters of sentiment. They are his only faults, I believe."

"Not serious," said Hanford, pleasantly. Then skilfully turning the conversation, he asked numberless questions about village celebrities. Some had been dead long, but Kathleen related with much animation events which had befallen the others, and their odd characteristics. Her clever descriptions and keen sense of humor compelled many pauses and much laughter, till it seemed to Hanford as they strolled on through sunshine and shadow as though a day were being lived over from the old days which his memory cherished so tenderly. Talk of individuals led to recalling old events, and many an excursion and adventure was laughed over and recounted.

"Do you remember, Miss Kathleen, that trip we took to Bowman's Pond for black bass, and how on the way over I stole a tintype of the Boston boy you had flirted with at boarding-school, and would not give it back because I declared that one beau at once was enough?"

"Indeed I do," laughed Kathleen.

"And how I put the picture in my coat pocket and left the coat beside the lunch basket on shore, while we went fishing in an old scow, and when we came back we found a tramp had stolen the lunch and my coat, too, so that I had to walk home in my shirt sleeves, and you laughed all the way, and declared that there was no honor among thieves because one thief had been robbed by another thief?"

Kathleen's laugh had the same old mischievous ring as she recalled Hanford's coatless figure.

"I've often thought of it," she said, breathlessly.

"What's become of the Boston boy, Miss Kathleen?"

"How should I know, Mr. Hanford; that was ten years ago."

"So you've forgotten him?"

"Ages ago."

"Have all your lovers shared that dreadful fate, Miss Kathleen?"

"I'm afraid they have," she answered, carelessly.

A sudden chill struck Hanford to the heart, but he gave no sign of emotion.

"No remembrance, and no pity, I suppose," he said.

"I have not observed that they need any."

The lake shore had been reached some minutes before, and they were now walking along the bluff, with Kathleen slightly in advance. It seemed to Hanford as he looked at the lithe, well-poised figure before him as though he could not give her up. All things in heaven and earth were shut out by one overmastering desire. Upon the highest point of the bluff four elms still stood just within the old, grass-grown earthworks. Under their welcome branches Kathleen and Hanford had many times found shelter in days gone by. Hanford made a seat with a mossy stone for the back for his companion, and threw himself on the turf at her feet. The memory of their last visit to the spot affected him powerfully, and perhaps even Kathleen recalled it, for she also was silent.

Already the declining sun had begun the close of a perfect day. The morning's sapphire blue of lake and mountain had vanished. Across the wide sweep of water lay an ever-moving pathway of gold, and beyond the far Adirondack peaks seemed clouded in a golden haze. Here and there a bit of white cloud relieved the deep blue of the sky. In the far distance to the south two blunt-prowed schooners were slowly tacking down the lake. The only sound that broke the stillness of the afternoon was the measured ripple of tiny waves along the rocky edge of the bluff.

Hanford broke the silence.

"Tell me of yourself," he said.

"There is little to tell," she answered. "I spent three years after you left in school and college, then two years in travel abroad, and since have lived quietly at home, occupied with household duties and occasional visits to Toronto, Washington and Boston."

"You make it an uneventful record, Miss Kathleen."

"It is."

"Hardly so colorless as that, I think. You know we used to be confidants," he added, smiling.

"Habits fallen into disuse for a decade cannot be lightly resumed, Mr. Hanford. Ten years mean change to us all. You, for example, changed many years ago."

Hanford colored at this thrust.

"You asked me about myself a little while ago, Miss Kathleen," he said gravely, "and I said little in reply. Now that you charge me with change, and thus have implied inconstancy,

it is but justice to myself to speak more freely
of my life than you have spoken of yours. I
grant that I have changed. I have attained a
man's estate in capacity for affairs, in knowledge
of life and in experience. In matters of heart
and sentiment no man was ever more true, un-
changed and unchanging. Ten years ago I left
this town bubbling over with a young man's
confidence and happiness. I had won your love,
though before I had not dared to hope for it, and
I had found the object of my professional research, thus insuring liberal reward. I intended
to bring the business part to a quick and happy
termination, and then to seek you and reach the
understanding not touched in our last talk. Alas
for human plans! I found my triumphant re-
port coldly received. Quarrels and death prevented further action, and I was not only cheated
out of my reward, but I could not collect my expense account and salary. Thus I suddenly found
myself with the tables completely turned, and
actually in debt. I cannot tell you of my suffer-
ings during the month I lingered in Boston. I
tried to make my letters to you cheerful and interesting, but their forced nature must have made
them hollow. About that time my mother died,
leaving my two younger sisters in my charge,
and when at length I had settled her affairs
and placed my sisters with a relative, guaran-
teeing their expenses, I found myself in New

York with but $11 in the world. I had no friends in the city, but I started out to find employment. My profession seemed filled. In no direction could I find an opening. Work I must and would. It came at length in humble form, and for five weeks, Miss Kathleen, I swept out a grocery store and delivered parcels. I cannot describe the discouragement and gloom of that period. It was then I failed to write you, and you chided me for neglect. Heaven knows your memory grew bright as my own perplexities and sorrows increased. Later I secured a humble position in a broker's office. It brought a mere pittance, but my sisters received their allowance without a break. They never knew what it cost me to send it. I lived practically in a garret, and for more than a year I ate meat but once a week, so rigidly did I economize. Do you wonder that when my poor, parched nature turned to far away Vermont and the girl I loved unfalteringly, and contrasted your luxurious surroundings and my own condition, that I grew sick at heart? 'Not yet,' I kept repeating, 'Not yet.' At length my employers began to notice my attention to duty and I was slowly advanced. It then became necessary to educate my sisters, for I determined they should have the advantages their birth demanded. My own debts, incurred unjustly for others, were still unpaid, remember, but I pushed steadfastly forward. Day and night I labored, and year by year I slowly advanced. Last month found me free of debt. One sister was married in June. The other is engaged, and is now, besides, self-supporting. As for myself, two weeks ago the firm made me a junior partner. I have taken no vacations beyond a day here and there with my sisters, and it all seems to me, as I look back upon it, one long, unending stretch of labor. During all this time my love for you was a thing apart from common life. Other women were nothing to me, and I kept saying to myself, 'When I am free I will go to Kathleen and tell her all.' "

Hanford's voice faltered and he paused a moment.

"You must not tell me this," said Kathleen, struggling to preserve her ordinary tone. She was unconsciously leaning forward toward Hanford, and nervously twisting a bit of grass to shreds.

"I must tell you," he said with an intensity that permitted no opposition.

"When at length my business affairs shaped themselves satisfactorily my thoughts turned to you, for at last I was free. Monday I determined to write you fully, and on returning to my apartment that evening I found the invitation to your wedding."

Again Hanford stopped as the recollection of that evening came over him.

Kathleen was silent. With parted lips and hands unconsciously folded, her eyes were fixed upon the far-away hills across the lake. Hanford's frank recital of his experiences and his unwavering devotion came like a revelation to her and affected her deeply.

"Of course my own hopes were entirely swept away by the news," continued Hanford quietly, "but one thought remained and that was of your happiness. I determined to take advantage of a northern trip to see you, and to ask a question."

"I cannot answer any questions, Mr. Hanford," interposed Kathleen, much agitated. "You have no right to ask them now, and I have no right to answer."

"The question was a simple one, Miss Kathleen. I felt that our relations in the past and my own unfaltering devotion to you gave me the right to ask it without presumption."

"I cannot answer your question, Mr. Hanford," she replied, "but after what you have just told me you are entitled to know more of my own life and thoughts than I have already explained. The story is not a long one, Mr. Hanford, nor is it pleasant. Do not delude yourself with the masculine idea that you have done all the suffering. It is the same old story, of a woman grieving in silence and alone, and maintaining an outward cheerfulness. Doubt, anxiety and sorrow, and their concealment, are not agreeable ten-year companions."

Hanford started at her unnoticed admission. Kathleen's tone was hard and bitter. Her face was pale, her hands tightly clasped. Long repressed emotions seemed struggling for the mastery.

"This is the final reckoning between us, Arthur Hanford," she continued more deliberately, "and you shall know the truth. When we parted ten years ago I loved you with all the earnestness I am capable of. I think few young girls of that age love with the fidelity and devotion that I did. You made the sad mistake of thinking my affection for you depended upon success. Why, I never thought of success. It would have been a mere incident, anyway. No true woman ever doubts her lover's ultimate success—whatever his present misfortunes—and if success never comes, her woman's heart merely grows tenderer and truer to console him in defeat. Your letters, so dear to me, became infrequent and they sounded hollow. My pride told me to write you as you wrote me, and only as often. As for my feelings, you must search your own suffering to understand mine. I finished school and entered college, but my heart was not in it. I was waiting and watching for one who never came. My thoughts were here. I lived over and over the days we had spent together. I read the books

we had read together. I have them yet. And
all this time I lived my life and took my part
in the events about me, and no one knew. No
one but my mother, she knew all. She urged
me to forget you. She said you were untrue,
and even if you were not you were unworthy
of me."

Kathleen paused. Hanford made no attempt
to answer. His face looked pale and drawn,
as though her simple story were an indictment
of his mistaken conduct too terrible to bear.

"I was not well for some time," continued
Kathleen, "and at the beginning of my second
year at college I became seriously ill. I was
taken from my studies and sent to Europe. Oh,
if you had only come to me then," she exclaimed
vehemently, as memory brought back the
thoughts of old.

"Kathleen," said Hanford, starting eagerly.

She regained her composure as quickly as she
had lost it.

"Too late," she said quietly. "No word came
from you. I was still true, but doubt and anxiety were usurping your place, and I was conscious of a growing sense of anger. My own
self-respect and pride were asserting themselves.
'What right has this man,' I kept saying, 'to
blast my life, and bring sorrow by reflection to
all who love me?' And so I arose, and shook
you off, Arthur Hanford, and began to do justice

to myself. Four winters ago, in the south of France, I met Colonel Ware. His attentions became marked at once. I did not encourage them, but, unlike many others in previous years, I did not discourage them. I longed for rest. The remaining years have been years of increasing happiness. I had shaken off the old life, and found a new one. I live in the present, Mr. Hanford, not in the past. That is folded up and laid away. I am blameless, unless, perhaps, I might be blamed for suffering so long. Not so with you. You were the master. You had the power of speech or silence. The meaning of each was plain. You chose silence. Perhaps you had wishes and hopes. Perhaps it was all a mistake. Well, the result is here before us. We cannot change it. If you still love me you must bear it to the end. You have brought sorrow on yourself and you have—you have"——

Kathleen faltered and stopped.

"I have what, Kathleen?" he demanded.

Again she recovered herself, and altered the sentence that was growing dangerous for her self-control.

"You have cut your own path, and you must walk in it."

Kathleen arose.

"And now, Mr. Hanford," she said in even tones, "we have had our explanations. You have told me what for years I hoped and dreamed and did not know. It comes too late, and I have told you—well, is it a pleasant thing to hear? The explanations are over. Have they profited either of us? Come, let us leave this place," she added vehemently.

Hanford did not rise. A sudden realization came over him that he had reached the end. The furtive, unnoticed hope which had buoyed him up on his journey fell away, and left a dreadful sense of error and failure through all his years of effort. Overwhelmed, he buried his face in his hands, and his strong frame shook convulsively.

No words of Arthur Hanford, had he pleaded till old age, could have spoken so eloquently to Kathleen Milbank as the bowed and quivering figure of the man she had loved so long and faithfully. Her self-control was swept away, and she kneeled beside him on the turf, an eager, anxious girl.

"Arthur," she cried, touching his arm, "you must not, you must not. Think of yourself—of—of me. We must not give way. I cannot stand it. Ask any question you wish, but please, please, be yourself."

With a great effort Hanford recovered his composure.

"The story of your life and mine makes one question just," he said. "The answer to it belongs to us both. Kathleen, do you love the man you have promised to marry?"

Her self-possession deserted her now.

"You should not ask that," she murmured, pale and agitated.

"I should ask it," he said, relentlessly. "Answer, on your soul. Do you love him, Kathleen?"

"He loves me far more than"——

Hanford arose and stood before her. "Kathleen Milbank," he said, speaking with an intensity that thrilled her, "if you love this man, no friend of yours will rejoice more earnestly at your happiness, or pray more unceasingly for its continuance than I. But if you cannot say you love him, as you and I understand the meaning of the word, you have no right to marry him, for if you do, you wrong him and you wrong yourself for life."

Kathleen was very pale. She made no effort now to go.

"I should not have come here with you," she said helplessly.

"Why?"

"Because I felt a strange certainty that you would bring this subject up."

"Why did you come, then, and did you dread this question?" asked Hanford.

Kathleen's will made one last stand.

"I cannot answer you, Mr. Hanford," she exclaimed.

He would not yield.

"Do you love him, Kathleen?" he urged.

No armor she possessed would keep that dreadful question out. There were traitors, too, within the citadel, for her own heart had often asked the question before. She hid her face in her hands to hide the rising color.

"Why have you come back," she exclaimed passionately, "you ruined my happiness for years, and as I struggle to regain it you snatch it away again."

"You are strangely inconsistent," said Hanford, quietly. "I said at the outset that if you really loved Colonel Ware my own feelings would sink instantly out of sight, and you should know me only as a loyal, steadfast friend. If I seem otherwise, why is it?"

Hanford waited a moment for a reply. None came.

"Kathleen," he continued deliberately, "you cannot meet the test. You do not love the man whom you are about to marry."

No answer. The silence that followed was broken only by a sob. It seemed to change them both.

"Does he know?" asked Hanford gently, at length.

"Yes," she whispered. "He says he can make me love him."

"And you thought he could?"

"Yes; I hoped so."

Hanford's voice sank to a whisper.

"Do you think so, now?" he asked.

Kathleen's slender figure trembled. She made no answer.

"Our mementoes of each other and the old days," Hanford went on without pressing a reply, "were not numerous, as you know, Kathleen, but I have one which has never left me, and for ten years has been the shrine of my heart. It is very precious to me, but I am going to return it to you now, for it may plead with you to do justice to yourself and to me."

He drew from his pocket a little worn leather case, and placed it in her hand. Kathleen opened it eagerly, and found within a wisp of withered goldenrod, clasped in a tarnished silver pin.

"Will you promise me on that token, Kathleen, that you will not marry any man you do not love?" Silence. It seemed to Hanford as though the beating of his heart drowned the ripple of the waves.

Kathleen raised her frank blue eyes to his.

"Yes," she said.

"Watson, J. D.?" inquired the messenger interrogatively, about midnight.

"Yes, fourth floor," answered the elevator man in no pleasant humor.

"Youse fellers," he said, as they went up, "is like flies. No sleepin' on account of yer. Thirty-seven," he added as he let the boy out of the car and went down again. The messenger knocked at 37.

"Telegram for Watson," he said.

There was a muffled sound within. Watson opened the door, and took the envelope. He tore it open and read:

"The common-sense Cupid won.   A. H."

"Watson's got a jag on," remarked the messenger to the elevator man five minutes later.

"What," exclaimed the latter in astonishment. "It's the first he's had in this house, then."

"Well, he gin me two plunks. If it tain't a jag, what is it?"

"It must be a jag," said the elevator man reflectively.

The Auction Bottle.

"You ain't the only one that's got left," said the station agent consolingly. "There's a man inside the station—little feller. Looks as though he mount be from Lewisville or Cincinnatty. Reckon you're from one of 'em yourself, ain't yer?" he added inquiringly.

"I'm from New York," I said, wondering vaguely if the station agent's flannel shirt hadn't reached the age limit which entitled it to be retired on a pension.

He was a man of perhaps forty years, of large frame and smooth-shaven face. One corner only of his wide mouth was utilized for purposes of conversation and expectoration, possibly to avoid the exertion of opening it all at once—a habit which imparted a whistling sound to the conclusion of each sentence.

There was a moment's silence while he inspected me with an evident accession of interest.

"Be you?" he said at length, "Well I'm sorry you got left, and now No. 3 is in trouble, too."

"What do you mean?" I asked anxiously.

"She's due at 9 o'clock, but I've just heard she's three hours late and gettin' later." With which comforting news he strolled away. With the next train three hours late and getting later, why hurry?

The feeble rays of a half-obscured October sunset were strugging across the station platform, along which I was aimlessly walking.

Enforced idleness is seldom pleasant to a busy man. I had missed my railway connections, and found myself angry but powerless on the platform of a little railway station in a sparsely settled mountain county of Eastern Kentucky.

Perhaps not the smallest factor in my discontent was the knowledge that I ought not to have attempted the trip at all. It was entirely my partner's suggestion.

"See here, Van Dunk," he said to me as we were discussing the firm's affairs one morning of the previous week, "Colonel Bibb objects to our bill for his book on 'Kentucky in the Rebellion.' He says $24 for alterations is outrageous; that the only alteration he made on the whole proof was to add an 's' to sassafras in the foot note on Page 19. He says that he won't pay the item. As a matter of fact, he tore his proof to pieces, and added and subtracted ad lib. Here is all the data and somebody ought to go and prove the thing to him."

"To Kentucky?" I asked incredulously.

"To Kentucky. We are always running up against alterations, and every case ought to be argued out with the customer."

"It strikes me," I remarked, "that it would be money in our respective pockets to yield the whole item and stay home. The amount involved is $24, and the trip would cost $75, leaving entirely out the time lost."

"Van Dunk," said my partner, impressively, "we are young men building for the future. For the sake of our reputation that item must be argued, and the Colonel convinced whatever it costs. My domestic affairs make it impossible for me to go. You are the man."

Peace must be preserved in the business family at all hazards, and I reluctantly started for a certain small out-of-the-way village in Kentucky, in no pleasant frame of mind, principally anxious to have the argument out with the military Bibb and return, and here I was within sixty miles of the Colonel's home and laid up indefinitely.

I looked off at the single track perspective, running drearily out to a point in the fast growing dusk, and tried to be as philosophical as the circumstances permitted.

There was absolutely no settlement about or

near the station, unless one house about three hundred yards away could be so dignified. The country itself was not unpleasing. The station stood on high ground that sloped gently to a small river, perhaps half a mile away, and easily seen. On the other side the country was rolling, broken and heavily wooded, the background of distant hills being sharply outlined by the setting sun. It was not exactly the place one would select for a long stay, and the chances for accommodation depended, it appeared, on the one house, where doubtless the agent resided.

The station itself lacked the customary sights and sounds. There were no engines, no belated freights, no arriving passengers and baggage. Not even the ever-present small boy disturbed the serenity of the October evening.

For a weary half hour I paced the platform, watching the shadows disappear and the dim outline of the river grow dimmer and fade. As the quiet became a bit oppressive, and the inner man began to make demands, I decided to consult the station agent about refreshments and possibly accommodations. The other passenger had evidently reached the same conclusion, for as I turned toward the waiting-room I confronted my fellow-unfortunate and the agent in conference.

"This is the other passenger," said the latter to me as I approached. "I just told him you 'uns could come over to my house to supper. It's the only house around here yet, and you can get a bite there, even if it ain't the Springs. Will you come?"

"With pleasure," I replied, noticing a strange but puzzling familiarity in the slight figure of the other passenger, who stood dimly outlined in the dusk. He was evidently struggling with the same problem, for he said suddenly:

"Aren't you Van Dunk, of New York?"

"I am, and you are"——

"Binney, pamphlet binder on West Broadway. Recollect, old man?"

I greeted him with a warmth that indicated my extremity. Although a small man there was enough of Binney to go a great way. He was one of those men whom you escape when you can, and regret it when you can't. I had always regarded him as a misfit in his calling. He was delicate, indolent and foppish, possessing a fondness for late hours and large rings, which fitted the prosaic and hustling requirements of a pamphlet bindery about as appropriately as a monkey at a funeral, and the continued existence and fair prosperity of his establishment were due largely to a plodding and faithful foreman, who did business when Binney did not, that is, most of the time.

"What on earth brings you here, Binney?" I asked in surprise.

"Business," he answered briskly. "Same with you, old man?"

"Yes," I gasped, trying to take in the thought that business could draw Binney from New York to Kentucky. It was too colossal to permit conversation at the same moment.

"It will be a good 10 o'clock before our train comes," continued the little man rapidly, apparently glad to get away from explanations. "And I was just going over to Mr. Todd's to get a bite. I'm mighty glad to meet a friend. So beastly unexpected, you know. Come along, old man."

The station master's house was a long, rambling, Kentucky farmhouse, which in one spot reached the dignity of two stories, and then relapsed again to one. He had been born in the house, he told us on the way over, and had always lived there, but the death of his mother about a year before had deprived him of his family relations and home life.

"'Tain't much there now," he said apologetically over his shoulder to me as we walked in single file along the rough road, thus intensifying the peculiar whistle with which he talked. "You see ma was a good hand about the house, but the gal I got to tend to me and John ain't no earthly good. I reckon she's better'n nothin', so she stays."

It seemed to me she was several degrees

worse than nothing, when I saw her, a few minutes later in the kitchen, where the evening meal was being spread.

An indescribable and accumulated odor of pork fat pervaded every nook and cranny of the long, low-studded apartment, and it seemed to have settled on the walls, the shelves and the dishes, as a sort of greasy grime. Amid these fragrant surroundings clattered a figureless female of uncertain age, with hair half fallen, and slippers half on, clapping the floor like bones at each step.

While she completed preparations for the supper Binney and I attacked the tin hand basin on the back porch, and then waited outside.

"There's beehives in the settin'-room," said the station master, as he joined us outside, and shut the door to drown the noise of frying. "Three of 'em was empty, and we put 'em in there for the winter. We don't use the room any more now ma's gone. Me and John is over to the station or on the farm most of the time." John appeared at that moment and announced supper. "The gal," having pitched the dishes on the table in utter confusion, was already seated herself, and eating when we entered. The station master took what seemed to be the head of the table, if one ignored the dishes, which were strewn more thickly about me than any one else, and John pushed the fried pork and boiled potatoes along to the host to serve. It would have been an interesting study to have watched little Binney's expression during the progress of the meal, had not a more interesting study been presented by "the gal." She sat impassive and unintelligent, unless a few furtive glances at little Binney's neatly curled mustache · could be called intelligent. With but one interruption, occasioned by a demand from the host for more potatoes, she devoted herself to a steady absorption of food, eating everything with her knife, except bread, which she ate with her fork, doubtless as a concession to the strangers present. The station agent seemed ill at ease, and though he made a remark or two during the meal, was inclined to be silent. John ate and said nothing, and fastidious Binney was so occupied and overwhelmed with a generous slab of salt pork that he seemed to have lost the power of speech. As for myself, I have knocked about enough to take the world as it comes, and devoted myself to a glass of milk, boiled potatoes and bread, reflecting with a good deal of sympathy upon the station agent's saddened life. The sorrow which deserves the most sympatny is that uncomplaining, unconscious sort which solicits none. Into this lonely Kentucky farmhouse Death had come and taken the mother and homekeeper away, but the son, unwilling to change from the

old way of life, pushed doggedly along, cher-
ishing ma's memory, and longing for the touch
of ma's hand, amid uncongenial associates who
intensified her loss. Nothing new about the incident but the sorrow of it, and sorrow is always new.

"Let's go back to the station," said Binney
abruptly, as we ended the meal. A suggestion
that both the station agent and I welcomed.

"Where'd you leave your satchel, Binney," I
inquired, as we started.

"Station."

"I have two," I said. "I left them in the waiting-room, and I hope no bear or wildcat has run
off with the little satchel, especially."

"Precious papers?'

"Precious liquid," I answered.

"Got a flask of brandy, old man?" asked little
Binney eagerly.

"Better than that."

"What do you mean, Van Dunk?" In his
eagerness he crossed the road and walked in
the dust so as to be at my side.

"I mean I've got a bottle of champagne in my
small satchel. Thought I might need it to cheer
up on in just such a scrape as this." The
transformation that occurred in little Binney
was marvellous.

"Old man," he said patting me affectionately
on the arm, as he walked beside me in the

dark, rising or sinking as he happened to strike a rut, "you're the most thoughtful man I ever heard of in my life. When shall we tap it, my boy?"

"Whenever you please," I replied, "provided you can procure ice and glasses of our friend, the agent."

The station agent was walking ahead of us, but he did not reach the station before Binney, and when I arrived I found the little man holding my small black waterproof satchel affectionately on his lap, and explaining the delights of a cold bottle to Mr. Todd.

"Open your satchel, Van Dunk," he said, eagerly. "Let's see the bottle."

It did not take long to satisfy that requirement, and little Binney fondled it as tenderly as if it had been a thing of life.

"You pull the cork out, and come up into the ticket office, and I'll get some cups," said the agent, eyeing the bottle with considerable curiosity and interest.

"Where's the ice?" asked Binney.

"What ice?"

"Why ice for the champagne, man."

"You don't need any."

Binney looked shocked.

"Champagne," he remarked, "must be cold or it's no good. Did you ever taste champagne?" he added.

"You can't tell a Kentuckian anything about liquor, sir," said the agent with dignity.

"Perhaps not, but champagne must be cold, or it loses its flavor and its life."

"Life; does it pop?" asked Mr. Todd, pityingly.

"Certainly."

"Sort of birch beer, hey?"

Binney gave a gasp of horror.

"Sir," he said solemnly, "this bottle contains the most sparkling, delicious, expensive and intoxicating beverage known in the civilized world."

"Is it anything like whiskey?" asked the agent incredulously.

"Far better."

"Does it corn yer?"

"One glass from that bottle, old man, and you'll think you own the whole State of Kentucky."

The agent looked relieved. "I'll git the cups," he said briskly, "bring her inter the office."

"Where's the ice?"

"We ain't got any."

Binney's face was a study. He looked at the bottle, at Mr. Todd and then at me.

"What shall we do, Van Dunk?" he asked appealingly. "Shall we go without ice, old man, or, or—not open it?"

"I haven't carried that bottle down from

Washington," I said with emphasis, "to drink the contents warm. Better put it up, Binney, and come outside for a walk on the platform with me," and to point the suggestion I strolled out into the cool October air, and began a leisurely promenade.

Little Binney did not follow, but a few minutes later the station agent came out.

"I reckon we can fix that," he said.

"How?"

"We'll ride over to the Casino at the Springs."

"What do you mean?" I asked, not especially pleased with a night trip to a rustic resort.

"Why, the Springs," he repeated, as though any one ignorant of that locality must be an idiot.

"The Casino over there is the finest saloon and eating house in America. Losin' a train is one thing, but great day'n morning, I ain't goin' to see a man git left on his bottle."

I didn't look enthusiastic.

"It's all right," he added reassuringly. "There is five hours before your train'll get here, and it's only eight miles over the mountain. John can work the wire and tend station while I'm gone, so I'll saddle up the three farm horses and we'll start right away. You kin git a ton of ice over there, Mr. Van Dunk," he called back, as he disappeared down the road toward his house.

"Isn't it elegant, old man?" said little Binney delightedly at my elbow.

"Well, not exactly elegant, but I'm willing. I'd like to see the Casino the agent talks about. What Springs does he refer to, Binney?"

"I don't know. Hang the Springs! Shall I carry that little black satchel of yours, Van Dunk?"

"Can you ride well?"

"Splendidly, old man." I avoided the decision of the satchel question, and a few minutes later we heard the tramp of hoofs, and the agent appeared riding a big white horse, leading two other steeds of passable appearance. I distrusted Binney's equestrian ability in spite of his emphatic statements, and so took possession of the precious satchel myself. The station agent procured a conductor's lantern, mounted his horse and led the way. I followed on one of the two other horses, and little Binney, perched on the third, a fat and broad-backed beast, brought up the rear of the strange cavalcade.

The clouds which had obscured the sunset had broken away. The night was still and clear, and through the tree tops of the woods into which we had almost immediately plunged, the stars shone with that exhilarating and inspiring clearness which follows a period of storm. If one's early years were associated with life in the saddle, no amount of grinding and vexatious office cares in a great city can destroy the early love, and though more years had passed than I liked to reckon since I had even mounted a horse, it was a delightful experience to find myself once more in the saddle. The distant office, with its perplexing cares of policy and finance, the pugnacious Bibb, and his bothersome bill of alterations, were all forgotten, and I gave myself up to the full enjoyment of the trip. The road which was rough and apparently little used, was level for the better part of two miles, then turned abruptly across a mountain brook, and led upward by sharp ascent through ever thickening woods over the hills seen dimly from the station. Of conversation there was little. The agent rode well ahead, and I should have been glad to have pressed him in speed had it not been evident that little Binney was already making his topmost pace. The riding was not good, and every now and then a groan from Binney indicated a tumble just escaped. Otherwise he had preserved a complete silence since the start, a phenomenon which indicated a serious state of affairs.

"Getting along all right, Binney?" I called back to him.

"Finely, old man," he answered, but the sentiment did not fit his feeble tones.

"I thought I heard you groan a few moments ago."

"You're mistaken. Must have been my saddle. It creaks like the deuce. Don't happen to have any oil in your satchel, do you, old man?"

"Where did you learn to ride, Binney?" I asked pretty well assured that this was his first lesson.

"Say, Van Dunk," he called back as though he had not heard my question. "How in the world do you happen to be toting that sample bottle of wine around down here? Are you subsidized to exhibit wine through Kentucky during October?"

"It's very simple," I said. "I started South via Washington; had a couple of hours there, strolled around the city, and happened to see a grocery selling out at auction. I always had a weakness for auctions, so I walked in and bid on that bottle, which I was paralyzed to find knocked down to me for eighty cents. There's the whole story."

"I wish they had auctions like that in New York," said Binney. "I'd hang around and bid"——

Another groan, followed by a howl of terror and a thud, and Binney's horse seemed to be running. Reining in my own beast, I sprang to the ground and caught the other horse, as it trotted placidly toward me.

"Are you hurt, Binney?" I called.

No answer.

Ahead, the station agent's lantern danced and glimmered among the trees. After several ineffectual calls our guide heard me and returned.

"What's wrong?" he inquired, as he saw me holding the two horses.

"Mr. Binney has had a bad fall. We must tie up the horses and hurry back to him. I hope he isn't badly hurt," I added, feeling rather anxious in spite of myself.

To be burdened with a wounded companion while travelling on horseback along a wild mountain road at night seemed about the last straw to that unique and troubled journey. Hastily tying the horses to trees, we hurried back, guided by the groans which Binney was now emitting with increasing frequency and force. By the dull light of the lantern we saw that he lay in a heap at the side of the road.

"Are you hurt, Binney?" I demanded.

"I am fatally hurt, Van Dunk," he whispered.

"Don't say that, my man; you're all right," I assured him as cheerfully as I could, but much alarmed at the turn matters were taking. Another groan.

"Send word to Mrs. Binney that I was trying to get through by horseback and was thrown in the woods in the dark and killed. Don't mention the wine part," he added, with a supplementary groan.

I was about to suggest an examination when a sudden breeze blew the lantern out.

Binney's groans were redoubled.

"Van Dunk," he gasped, "it is gettting very dark. I have only a few minutes to live. There's something I must tell"——

"Here, here," I said briskly, "of course it's dark, the lantern's out. As soon as Todd lights up we are going to look you over."

A moment later, amid a volley of groans, I stretched the huddled form of my fellow-townsman and traveller at length in the road, regardless of mud, and anxiously sounded his vital parts.

"Is your head hurt, Binney?" I asked as I felt around for a gaping wound.

"It's not the head."

"Is it the chest?" I asked, transferring my investigations.

"I think it is."

I loosened his clothing and felt him over carefully.

"Did the horse step on you?"

"Lord, yes; all over me."

"I don't think your chest is hurt, Binney," I said at length, failing to find even a scratch.

"Perhaps not." His tones were slightly stronger. "I think it is the hips, Van Dunk. I have dislocated both legs."

With this pointer I went to work in that direction, and heedless of protests, punched, kneaded, slapped and worked every joint in his body.

"Get up, Binney," I said at length.

He sat up.

"Is it anything serious, old man?" he asked.

"Nothing whatever. You slid off the horse, and likely sat down hard on a rock. That's all. Come, get your beast."

"Sat down hard," he said groaning at the recollection. "I can never sit down again. Oh, Van Dunk," he added in genuine anguish as he slowly came to his feet, "you don't know how I feel. One boil growing on top of another boil and hit with a club, don't express it."

"Shall I telegraph your wife?" I inquired.

Binney seemed to improve suddenly.

"The trouble with that horse is he's so wide I can't get any purchase on him," he said. "How will you swap horses, old man?"

Anything for peace. The station agent and I helped Binney on my horse, and the procession started again. This time with Binney in the middle. The road from the summit down the other side seemed more trodden and was much smoother. With no mishaps, therefore, we reached the valley, and, turning to the left, a glimmering of distant lights told of our approach to some settlement. The road was now excellent, and quickening our pace we were soon riding through a small town, apparently lying picturesquely between hills. The village itself seemed to consist largely of cottages and hotels, marking it at once as a fashionable resort. We had evidently crossed the State line, and this was doubtless one of the innumerable mineral spring resorts in the Virginias. The main street, which was lined with villas, ran along a narrow river, the same, so Todd informed me, as the one that I had seen from the station. Across the river, which was spanned by a rustic bridge, and on the high bank opposite, stood a large and brilliantly lighted building, with towers and a promenade extending some distance along the crest of the hill, above the river. This was our objective point, the long-sought Casino. The promenade was hung with Chinese lanterns and dotted with colored electric lights, imparting an exceedingly festive air to the scene. Although October, the chill of the Northern fall was lacking, and people were to be seen in every direction with but light wraps, enjoying the festive scene and the music which came softened from one of the towers. Little Binney forgot his wounds, and, cantering up to me, exclaimed: "Isn't this great, old man; biggest adventure of my life, Van Dunk."

Before reaching the bridge the station agent halted, and we surrendered our horses to be stabled.

"What is your plan?" I asked a few moments later, when he rejoined us.

"It's just this: Take that gripsack of yours right up to one of them tables in the Casino, call a nigger, and tell him to open the bottle for three gentlemen. I ain't ever been in there before, and now, if we've got a bottle of the best stuff in the world, I'd like to let 'em know it."

I couldn't help feeling amused at the proposition, though not overanxious to appear in a fashionable resort, unkempt myself and with my unique companions. No better plan, however, suggested itself at the moment, and little Binney settled the matter by saying: "It's a good scheme, old man. I'll stand the corkage myself. Let's move along."

Accordingly we walked across the bridge, and climbed the stairway that led to the general promenade. I walked ahead and carried the satchel, and in consequence did not notice the attention we were attracting; but when we reached the main building and entered the restaurant the full glare of the brilliantly lighted room fell on my two companions with paralyzing effect. For a moment I wondered whether we would be admitted. The station master, with his stalwart frame incased in a flannel shirt of unknown antiquity, bearing the grime of the day's toil upon him and the newly acquired fumes of the stable about him, was embarrassing enough in a fashionable meeting-place, where evening dress was seen on all sides. But he was as nothing to little Binney.

There is a tradition in my family that in childhood I found a pot of yellow paint in the stable, and industriously daubed my little sister from head to foot, and then proudly presented her to my mother's horrified gaze with the triumphant announcement that I had brought her a little canary. This tale I have always denied, but if true, that mite of a girl in yellow could not have looked more demoralized than little Binney as the glare of the lights fell full upon him. There was mud everywhere except on his collar, which had completely disappeared beneath the horizon. The back of his mud-besprinkled coat was torn from the collar to the pocket; his face was streaked, his hair on end, and the luxuriant mustache so carefully watched and tended had yielded to the killing dampness of the woods and drooped mournfully over his mouth. All unconscious of his appearance, little Binney was enjoying every moment. He evidently believed that the attention he attracted was a tribute to his metropolitan air and manners. My own appearance I well knew could not be reassuring, and I hastily led my motley companions to a table in an alcove adjoining the large dining-room, from which we could look out on the animated scene. The myriad lights, the waltz music from the band in the tower just beyond, the buzz of laughter and conversation, and the hurrying waiters flitting from table to table made a vivid picture long to be remembered. The station agent gazed upon the gay scene with open-mouthed admiration. Suddenly he leaned over to me and whispered:

"I want to see the boss."

"What's the matter?"

"Them niggers is hurryin' too much. They'll drop the dishes sure as you live. I never seen a nigger hurry yet that he didn't spile what he was doin'. It's unnatural for a nigger to hurry."

Little Binney had been slowly recovering from the shock of sitting down, and the reference to waiters brought him to himself.

"Don't mind the dishes," he said, irritably. "We didn't come across the mountains to save dishes. Where's the satchel, Van Dunk?"

I called the head-waiter, who was passing, and said:

"There's a quart bottle of champagne in this little satchel. I wish you would take it and have it served properly. My friends and I have come across the mountain on purpose to drink this particular bottle together, well served."

The head-waiter looked at the unkempt station agent and little Binney's streaked but eager countenance in dignified surprise, but he took the satchel, and the auction bottle seemed at last about to be uncorked.

"How does it happen to be so gay over here and so deserted on your side of the mountain?" I asked the station agent, to distract his thoughts from the waiters, whom he was still watching with alarm.

"'Taint a pleasant story," he answered short-ly. "My station was put in to reach the springs, and the wagon-road cut through across the mountain, and when we got it started and it looked like there'd be a town around the station in six months, blamed if some fellers didn't build a branch railroad from South Forks right inter the town and it left my station clean out. That's how."

I did not answer, for I saw my little black satchel approaching, borne in a gingerly manner by a small colored man.

"Is this yours, sah?" he asked.

"It is."

"De wine am clean gone, sah."

"What do you mean, man?"

"De cork had popped and de wine was all out in de gripsack, sah."

The brand was the best. For a moment I felt utterly bewildered. As nearly as I could recol-lect it was perfectly corked and wired.

"The wire seemed cut, sah," suggested the waiter.

A sudden thought flashed through my mind. I looked across the table at little Binney, blink-

ing and dilapidated. His sheepish look and tell-
tale silence were enough.

"Binney," I said, sharply, "did you cut that
wire?"

"Yes," he said, humbly.

"When?"

"After you left the station."

"What did you do it for?"

"I wanted to drink it, anyway, Van Dunk, ice
or no ice, and I just cut one wire; the other was
there. I don't see how it popped. I'm dreadfully sorry, old man, indeed, I am." His voice
quavered mournfully out and left him on the
verge of collapse.

The station agent glared at Binney in silence.
His looks expressed it all. It was fortunate his
anger took that form, for had he whistled out
a few picturesque Kentucky phrases they would
have insured our immediate ejection.

I was conscious of an overwhelming sense of
irritation at my meddlesome fellow-passenger.
He had no right to touch the bottle I had carried
down from Washington with so much care, and
now, through his officiousness, I had lugged an
empty flask at infinite inconvenience in the
dark.

"It's a fine satchel," said the station agent at
length, his professional instinct aroused. Not a
drop was spilled. I never see the like. Last
spring a can of preserves was busted in the bot-

tom of a trunk I was puttin' on the baggage-car of Number 2, and the juice come out on my shirt so I reckon I smelt like I was a quince for a week."

The story was doubtless true. The stains were still in evidence.

Little Binney paid the corkage, and had I not been well convinced earlier in the trip that he was much cramped financially I should have insisted on generous reparation. As it was, the situation was embarrassing; for while I would gladly order a new supply of champagne for the station master, I was determined that Binney should not receive any such attention at my hands. I was disgusted with the whole trip; regretted that I had consented to make it, and felt anxious to return immediately.

"Waiter," said I, decisively, "bring a bottle of beer and a plate of cheese sandwiches, and bring them quick."

The station agent looked horrified. A bottle of whiskey and three glasses he could have understood and approved, but beer was a strange and watery drink. This sentiment, however, he modified on its arrival, and when, an hour later, I insisted on our departure, both the station agent and little Binney were feeling like property-owners. It was 9:30 when, with many groans, little Binney was again in his saddle, and we turned toward the hills. The little binder was especially voluble, and, after we had progressed a mile or two, he developed an unpleasant habit of stopping his horse, twisting around in his saddle and apologizing profusely for the wire episode. We lost so much time by this diversion that the station master was far ahead and the glimmer of the lantern died suddenly away.

"Shut up, Binney!" I called, angrily, as he began the sixth apology. "You're completely in the dark. Your horse may stumble, and if he does, it will be serious for you."

In fact I felt considerably alarmed. We were now in the thickest part of the forest. Occasionally a star glimmered for a moment overhead, but it was blackest night below. Although the horses moved cautiously along, we were absolutely at their mercy, and my companion, who on such a journey needed more than his faculties when at their best, was semi-intoxicated. Sharp words and his own fears, however, did much to sober him, but our progress at best was exceedingly slow. It seemed to my excited senses that we had travelled hours, and I was beginning to fear we had strayed from the road, when I caught the distant glow of a light apparently stationary. The horses quickened their pace, and in a few minutes we had reached the station master's lantern, standing in the middle of the road. His horse was tied to a neighboring tree, and he himself sat on a fallen stump, apparently in great pain.

"What's the trouble?" I asked, in alarm.

"It's the first time, and, by gum, it's the last!" he ejaculated.

"What do you mean?"

"That beer. Idea of asking a Kentuckian to take a sickly, watery drink with suds on top, and I'm just where I orter be. Sick. Sick, I tell you. Sick as an old cow," he moaned.

"Can't you ride?" I asked, sympathetically.

"Ride?" he paused to double up with another paroxysm, "ride? "I'd rather die!"

"But man, we must catch that train."

"Ketch it."

"And leave you here?"

"Certainly. Take the lantern and get out. I'll wrastle it out with the beer and come home in the morning. John'll take the horses, or you kin—— Great day 'n mornin', there it comes again!"

I disliked to leave Mr. Todd in such a plight, but compromised by giving him a small bottle of brandy carried for just such emergencies, and when Binney and I resumed our journey with the lantern it was already after 11. We therefore pushed forward with increased speed, in spite of the roughness which characterized that end of the road, and at twenty minutes before 12 we drew up at the station platform.

I must confess it was with a feeling of profound relief that I sprang from my horse. I presume Binney was equally relieved. He had said nothing for at least three miles. One dim light glimmered from the station, which seemed utterly deserted, in the midst of a wilderness. I hastened around to the waiting-room entrance. The room was dark and empty. The single light I have mentioned came from the ticket office. I opened the door and stepped in. John was asleep on two chairs.

"Wake up!" I exclaimed. "When will the train be here?"

"Where's Todd?" he asked, vacantly.

"He's sick in the woods," I answered. "When will the train be here?"

"What train?"

"Number three, I think you call it, when is it due, man?"

"Number three went through at half-past ten."

"What?" I gasped.

The intellectual John bunched up his coat for a pillow, and laid down again.

"Yes," he said drowsily. "Wildcatted through."

I didn't wait to hear his snores resumed.

"Binney," I called in despair, hastening out on the platform. "What do you think has happened? While we fooled our time away over there at the Springs, that train has come and gone. It passed here at half-past ten. What on earth"——But Binney didn't answer. He was curled up on the baggage truck asleep.

The Unauthenticated Serpent.

"You're about the only man," he said slowly, "that ever asked what his first name was."

"Why is that?"

"Well, sir, I never knew why. He was just 'Walker' to everybody. Always was, from a boy. I knowed him from a little chap at school, and he was just Walker, then. His name was Edward, but bless your soul, there wa'n't a dozen folks in Wyoming County knew it, and after awhile it did seem like the Edward sort of mildewed off, from lack of use, and left him plain 'Walker.' "

I was a stranger on the lake, and I had idly asked the weather-beaten old fellow fishing from a flat-bottomed scow near me who kept the time-worn hotel which stood on the further shore. My neighbor's luck had been no better than mine, and he was quite willing to talk.

"Yes," he said reflectively, "it's Walker's,

Walker is dead, but it's Walker's Hotel. It always has been and it always will be, I suppose, till it burns down or dries up. I reckon," he added, after a pause, "that no other house in America was ever built in the way that was."

"How was that?"

"Perhaps you never heard of the Great Sea Serpent of Silver Lake?"

"I never did."

"Well, the sea serpent built that house, and he built it well. It's stood forty years just as you see it now."

"What was the sea serpent?"

"Well, it all happened before the war. They talk about jokes and schemes and fakes, as they call 'em, nowadays, but that snake was the all-firedest biggest hoax ever heard on in these parts."

"Do you know the story?"

"Know the story?" echoed the occupant of the scow, looking compassionately at me across the water. "Man and boy I've lived here sixty years, and I was in that job from beginning to end. Mebbe you'd like to hear about it?" he added inquiringly.

"I certainly should," I replied, with a sense of satisfaction that the lake might be made to produce some compensation for poor fishing. The old fellow let out his anchor a turn or two, swung around my way, and after putting on a fresh bait he began:

"In 1855 my father owned a farm along the western shore of the lake. If we was a bit further out you could see some of the medder land, just round the point over there. I was a likely young feller in those days, and there wasn't much about this lake I didn't know. It wasn't like it is now around here. To be sure there were picnics and all that in the summer season, but there wasn't a house on the lake shore from end to end, except the old hotel of Walker's, and the water was alive with fish. In the spring of '55 I was twenty-one; I reckon Walker was about twenty-eight. Walker was a curious feller, one of them quiet, deep sort of men. The Perry village people hadn't thought he was very heavy-headed, but since 1855 I hain't seen a man in the whole town of Perry that could have kep' up with Walker in solid brains.

"His father had died the year before, and left him a farm just back from the lake and a good piece of land along the shore with an old hotel and picnic grounds. The Walker family was supposed to run the hotel in the summer and sort of farm it the rest of the time. But Walker wasn't satisfied with that. Si Blodgett and I was his best friends, and he used to talk to us of how things was goin' and wish he could stir 'em up. Si lived next to me up on the West Road. One night early in June Si and me rowed over to Walker's. I could row across the lake in those days quicker than I can now. Well, Walker had been doin' chores around that old hotel, getting ready to open it up for the season, and I tell you it looked dismal enough in the dusk. He seemed to have something on his mind.

" 'Boys,' sez he, 'I'll lock up here and then you can come down to the boathouse with me awhile; I've got something to talk to you about.' He locked up the hotel and we three went down to the lake shore. I never see'd a prettier night than that was; there wasn't a cloud in the sky nor a ripple on the whole blessed lake, and every star shone up from the water as though it was sky above and sky below. We sat down on a bench by the boathouse.

" 'I've got a plan in my head, boys,' said Walker, 'that's a pretty serious one. I want to know whether you two will stand by me to the end?'

" 'Walker,' says Si Blodgett, 'we three was brought up together; if you want any help from us, we're with you till you say no.' Then I told him about the same thing.

" 'Well,' he said, 'I knew we three hadn't been friends for nothing, but I've reached a place where I've got to make a big move of some kind or go under. What with a poor season last year and father's death, I don't mind telling you it's as much as I can do to hold on to the farm and

hotel. I thought of working the farm and trying to rent the hotel, but I could not see enough
in that to pull me through. Fact is, boys, there's
only one chance; I need ready money for the
mortgages, and if the hotel has a good season
I'm all right. I've been thinking and thinking
how to make sure of that sort of season, and
I've got an idea about it. You see this is a
little lake; it's out of the way and not much
known, and people come to fish and picnic, but
the hotel don't draw much business. Boys, an
ordinary season won't pull me through; I want
a sensation, and I've got to get one or smash.
Last winter I read an article in a newspaper
about the sea serpent being seen in Long Island
Sound, and how city people just poured into the
towns around there and kept up a big excitement. Now, Si Blodgett, why can't we have a
sea serpent right here in Silver Lake?'

"Walker was excited. He talked low and
quiet, but I tell you he was worked up. Well,
sir, it fairly took the breath out of Si Blodgett
and me. I think Si nearly fell off the bench.
'Wouldn't it be found out?' he asked, sort of
shaky.

" 'Not if it's worked right.'

" 'How's that?'

" 'My idea is to have the serpent appear pretty
often at first, and get people excited and coming to the lake, and then we can stop when
they get too thick.'

"Si Blodgett didn't seem to think much of the plan.

" 'I'll tell you what, Walker,' said he, soothingly, 'I'll do anything to help you, but this is dangerous for us all. You want to rig up a log or something, and get people all by the ears, and then when they're worked up they'll find us three down in the marsh pulling a big wooden snake around with a string. I tell you, Walker, they'll tar and feather us.'

" 'You're right, Si,' said Walker, just as quiet as you please. 'If we had a lame plan like that, we might as well go to jail beforehand. I've got a safe plan all laid out; listen to it, boys, and then I'll leave it to you whether we try it or not.'

"Well, sir, Si Blodgett and I had always been fond of Walker, but till he began to talk that night we never knew what a head there was on him. He had the whole thing planned out. His serpent was to be a big hosepipe, painted dark green, with white spots. There was to be a keg at one end, made over to resemble a big serpent's head, and painted a bright color. The critter was to be raised by air and sunk by water, and operated from the shore by a small pipe which should be connected with the tail of the snake. Walker's idea was that as the hotel was but a few rods from the lake, the piping should be run underground to the house,

and then up to a room which commanded a good
outlook and from which the whole thing could
be operated.

"The trouble seemed to be to move the thing
around, but Walker said that when it was on
the surface and full of air it would be easy to
work about, and a coil of light rope connecting
from the snake to the other shore and then
back over a pulley, and another line from the
other side, would do. Well, he drew such a
vivid picture of the whole thing, the snake's
appearance, the fright of the people on the lake,
the newspaper accounts and the crowds that
would come, that when he ended by saying:
'Now, boys, there's the plan. I said I would
leave it to you, and I will. What do you say to
it?' neither Si Blodgett nor I hesitated a second. We were really only boys. We jumped off
that bench by the boathouse and told him we
would go in heart and soul, and swore by all
our old friendship to stand by him to the end.

"Well, sir, at that Walker almost broke down,
and I began to see how much depended on it
for him. We settled that evening what each
of us was to do. Walker had about $100 in
money, which he thought would get the hose
and fittings, and he was to go to Buffalo for
them by the end of that week. We arranged
while he was gone that Si and I should make
the head and a strong bellows in a vacant loft

over my father's toolhouse. The fitting together could only be done in Walker's barn at
night. We concluded ten days would be enough
for that part of the work and that we could be
ready for business about July 6. It was so late by
this time that Si and I said a hurried good-night.
and started across the lake. I shall never forget that trip. In our excited state every shadow was the dim outline of a sea serpent, every
ripple the beginning of a head. Well, sir, for a
week off and on as we got the chance, without exciting any attention, Si and I worked
away on that head, and I tell you we fixed up
the reddest and awfullest-looking critter you
ever see. We wrapped it up in sacking and
rowed it over the lake one quiet night about
the end of June. We took it right up to the
loft in Walker's barn, where he was collecting
all his material. He cut off the sackin' and
took a look at the head. You should have seen
how pleased he was.

" 'Boys,' says he after a minute, 'it almost
makes me shiver. That head will pull Wyoming County clean out of its boots.'

" 'Well,' says I, 'if that head hadn't been
wrapped up coming over in the boat, and them
eyes had been out a-lookin' at us, I reckon Si
Blodgett and I would have fell overboard.'

"Si and I spent that night with Walker, and
we put in some work on the critter, I can tell

you. Walker had bought a lot of things in Buffalo piecemeal, and so no one up there was suspicious. As he was getting the hotel ready for summer, Perry people didn't think anything about the bundles that kep' a-comin'. I reckoned he'd have some trouble gettin' the hose, but somehow Walker's luck was always stiddy. He found just the thing. It had been made for a hose company up in the city and rejected because it was too large for them. It was about a foot thick, made of leather, closely riveted. Most hose like that is stiff and heavy, but this was limber and just about the right weight. There was twenty-four feet of that hose, and Walker had painted it green, and mottled it up some with white paint. Well, sir, we fitted the head on and got the critter pretty well into shape that night. The connecting air pipe was left until the last thing. The critter was the first step. The next thing was laying the pipe. Walker said he would attend to that, to prevent suspicion, and Si and I set the pulleys on the east shore. That was no easy job. Walker was always sayin', 'Boys, do everything so well that you won't be afraid of gettin' found out if the whole of Wyoming County camp out along the lake'; and Si and I set those pulleys into rock under water and then arranged brush and stone over the place along shore. We did it all at night, and if we hadn't set marks we never in the world could have found those pulleys again.

"Walker himself pegged away at them pipes, and I tell you it was a job. He laid two pipes side by side underground from a swampy place down on the lake shore, a little way below the hotel, right up to the cellar and then up the east chimney, that being boarded up, to the southeast room on the second floor. The air pipe was small, but the other pipe, which was intended to carry the cords to operate the critter, was a two-inch tubing, and strong.

"Walker was anxious to have things all ready by the Fourth of July, because that always brought a crowd to the lake, but it was no use tryin' for that. I never see'd a scheme with so much solid work in it. Si and I was busy round the farms all day, and I tell you when we got through with our night work besides we was petered out. By the 10th of July we was about ready. Si and I was pretty excited when we rowed over that night. We each had a bundle of clothes with us, as Walker had hired us to help at the hotel for a couple of weeks—at least that was the story we told. It was a hard time for both of us to get away, bein' right in the busy season, and my father kicked like a mule about it, but I went just the same.

"That night we sort of put things together. We connected the bellows and air pump with the air pipe, after blowing a small plug through the other tubing. To the plug was fastened a string, and with that we pulled through all the cords, carefully soaped to make them move freely. It may seem sort of unlikely to you that there was any chance of moving this big critter around as we expected to do, and controlling it from such a distance, but it really was not. Walker had such a head on him that he had all the details figured out. His plan was just this: A small leaded rubber pipe, and plenty of it, connecting the air pipe on the shore with the middle of the serpent. This made it easy to raise or lower the serpent at will, water being admitted when the air pressure was removed by a suction valve in the side of the hose. In the other tubing were five cords, one at each side of the head, leading forward, but to opposite shores, and one at each side of the tail, leading the other way. Another cord connected with the head so as to give that an independent motion. Then the work was finished, but night after night we watched and waited for one that was dark enough to be safe. At last on the 16th there came up a hard northeast storm.

"That night was as dark as a pocket, and I tell you, sir, there were three excited men around Walker's Hotel. About 11 o'clock we crept out to the barn and took the serpent down to the shore, connected the pipes with great care, and Si Blodgett and I towed the snake out to the spot agreed upon. Walker hurried back to the hotel; he was to signal with a light from the southeast room when we were to cast the critter off. We had hardly reached the spot when he gave the signal and we cut loose. Although the night was so dark, we were close enough to the serpent to see it lying on the surface of the lake beside us. The head rode high in the water, being of wood, and those horrible eyes glared straight ahead.

"Minute after minute passed. Each one seemed an hour. The snake's position showed not the slightest change. Was it a failure after all? Si Blodgett and I were so excited that we breathed with difficulty. Suddenly I heard Si's hoarse whisper: 'Hen, the head is sinking.'

"It surely was. Little by little it lowered into the lake until the water rippled over the eyes. Then down the whole dark and mottled length there was a convulsive tremor, so lifelike that it was hideous, and the snake appeared to be moving toward us. The head arose out of the water and swayed slightly from side to side. I never expect to see a more horrible sight than that critter presented. I knowed all about it; I had made that head myself; but I jumped back to my seat, and rowed for the shore till both oars bent. The Great Sea Serpent was in the lake, a reality at last.

"That night Walker, Si Blodgett and I had a long discussion about the serpent's public appearance, and we agreed to let it be seen only at night until we were accustomed to working it. Walker was the proper man to operate the critter, but, of course, he had to be about the hotel and be very careful not to excite suspicion, so he gave Si Blodgett the key of that southeast room and put him in charge. I was to be the outside man, loafing around on the lake, fishing or rowing, near where the serpent was, and ready with a set of signals in case of any trouble. The next day was bright and sunny and we all worked quietly around the house. About suppertime five or six young fellows from Perry drove up to the hotel. One of 'em was Lon Scribner, who worked for the newspaper that came out every week at Perry. Walker gave me a look, and then he went to meet 'em.

" 'How's the fishin', Walker?' says Lon.

" 'First rate.'

" 'Let us have a boat for a couple of hours?'

" 'Glad to,' says Walker.

"They got out and hitched, and Lon, says he: 'Where are the bass bitin' this year, Walker?'

"Walker sat down on the horse-block and thought about it. 'Well,' says he, 'I haven't been out much myself, but I hear the best place is over east of the inlet. You might try it there.'

"I knew what was coming. The serpent lay just east of the inlet.

"They started out, and I told Walker I thought I would go fishing myself. So I rowed slowly over a ways, and kept watch on the party. It was about 9 o'clock when they came over by the inlet. It was time for the serpent. I lit my pipe and rowed slowly along. The light was the signal to begin. The fishing party had been having good luck before, but they were perfectly quiet for about five minutes, then Joe McKnight said: 'Guess we're driftin', ain't we, Lon?'

" 'No, we ain't.'

" 'Well, there's a big log over there.'

" 'Can't be,' says Lon.

"There was a silence, and then Joe McKnight said in the scaredest voice I ever heard, 'Boys, that thing is moving!'

" 'It's bendin' round!' says one of the others. 'There's a head on it! Great heavens, look at those eyes!'

"Well, sir, there was all creation let loose in that boat. Those fellows just fell over each other to get at the anchor, and they lost their knives in the water trying to cut the rope. They pulled and cussed and shouted, and all the time Lon Scribner was calling loud enough to be heard a mile, 'Pull, pull, or we'll all be killed!'

"Well, they did pull. I never seed a boat move

so fast before, and in five minutes they landed by a medder on the east side, and left the boat there, and walked home. The next morning Lon Scribner came over for the wagon, and before noon the newspaper man come over to see Walker.

" 'Mr. Walker,' says he, 'there was a terrible occurrence on the lake last evening.'

"What's that?' says Walker, lookin' surprised.

" 'A monster of the deep, sir, pursued a party of young men.'

" 'Hoax, isn't it?' said Walker.

" 'I thought so myself at first, but I have the sworn statement of every man in the party.'

" 'What did it look like?'

" 'They describe it, sir, as an enormous serpent, of horrible appearance, fully fifty feet long, with a head as large as a cow, and immense, fiery eyes.'

" 'Well,' said Walker, 'I hope it isn't true. It'll stop fishin' and ruin my business if it is, but the fact is I shouldn't be surprised if queer things turned up in the lake now and then. You know that place where they've never been able to find bottom?'

" 'Yes,' said the newspaper feller, anxiously.

" 'Well, my father always declared that was an underground outlet to Lake Ontario.'

"The newspaper man made a note of that.

Then he went down to the boathouse and looked about; and you should have seed the newspaper he turned out two days after that. There was a picture of a tremenjous snake printed on the first page, and eight columns of readin' matter about the monster in Silver Lake, with afferdavits from ten or fifteen people who had seed it. Well, sir, Walker give one glance at that paper and then he sent word over to Perry for a big lot of provisions and rowed down the lake himself and bought up every rowboat at the south end.

" 'Now, boys,' says he to Si and me, when he got back, 'watch out sharp, the crowd'll be here to-morrow.' An' it was. There's no use makin' a long story 'bout the people, but I never seed the like of 'em. The population's growed in forty years, and that education business over there in the grove, and the cottages and whatnot brings a crowd here every summer nowadays, but I tell you they're just nothin' to the slathers of people that poured around this lake for five weeks in the summer of '55. They come in wagons, they come a-foot. There was single men and women and whole families. I reckon there were 500 people camped out every clear night through August. The roads all about were lined with teams askin' the way to Silver Lake, and had they caught the serpent?

"As for Walker, he just tended hotel night

and day stiddy. He run his prices up out of sight, but it didn't make no difference. There was a crowd a-beggin' and quarrellin' for rooms all day long, and as fer boats, they was 50 cents an hour, and even then the crowd at the boathouse had to draw lots fer next chance. Walker wasn't the only one, though, that was workin' that serpent. The newspaper man was nearly crazy; along in the spring the Sheriff had been lookin' fer him on a judgment, but by the middle of August he had hired a crowd of men and bought two more printing presses. Every other day he run out a sea serpent extra, with cuts and big headlines. It wasn't Wyoming County alone, though, that was broke up over that serpent. The postmaster at Perry was about wild with letters from everywhere askin' was it real. He got 'em from New England and Pennsylvania, and two from Kentucky in one day.

"As fer the serpent, I tell you we was cautious. Up to the latter part of August we had let it appear ten or a dozen times, mostly at night. Twice the thing had been seen in the daytime by people on the shore; somehow it happened no one was on the lake at the time, and I will say that a more lifelike critter I never see. I didn't blame the fellows that walked around and swore to that snake. I'd almost swore myself.

"Well, about the first of September the excitement was so great it began to get hot. Over in Perry they formed a company with a capital of $1,000. They called it the Experiment Company, and the members swore they'd ketch that snake, dead or alive. The president and secretary went to Buffalo to consult fishermen and divers, and three days afterward they come over to Walker's bringin' a tall feller with chin whiskers and a harpoon. Blamed if he wasn't a whaler, and the company had imported him from Nantucket. They bought a boat and that whaler sat there on the lake all day with his harpoon on his arm.

"The day after that feller came the crowd was twice as big, just to see the whaler, I reckon. Walker began to look worried. Well, about 1 o'clock the next day a Rochester man turned up with a tremendjous iron fish hook, an old clothesline and two live hens.

"Everybody laughed fit to kill, but he didn't. He hired a boat, rowed out on the lake and somehow drifted over east of the inlet. Then he stuck one of them squawkin' chickens on his hook and dropped it over. About ten minutes after that the feller give a screech, and there he was, a-hangin' to the clothesline, and it was pullin' his boat along! The effect of that screech was wonderful. People on the shore ran along the bank and shouted like Indians, and all the

boats on the lake rowed like mad fer the man
with the hook. The whaler led the pack, stand-
in' up in the bow of his boat with the harpoon
ready. Just then the fisherman's boat slacked
up, and he stood up with a piece of cord in his
hand. The clothesline had broken. I almost
fainted, I was so scared, but I hurried over to
the hotel and found Walker. He was most
crazy. We went up to the southwest room and
had a hurried conference. It seemed that Si,
seein' that fisherman rather too close to where
the serpent was, had tried to shift the critter,
and must have caught the hook by doing it.
The snake begun to work badly just before the
clothesline broke, and I tell you it didn't break
a minute too soon.

" 'Boys,' says Walker, decidedly, 'it's gettin'
too hot; the snake has served its purpose; we've
made enough money to pull me out of trouble
and do the handsome thing all around. Now
we'll end the whole thing.'

"Si and I agreed. We were ready enough to,
bein' a little scared. By good luck that night was
stormy. After midnight we three went out on
the lake, found the pulley connection on the
other shore, and hauled up the serpent. Sure
enough there was that Rochester feller's hook
and chicken wedged round the hose near the
critter's head. The hook had picked a hole in
the leather and so the serpent was damaged

anyway. We towed it out to the place where they have never touched bottom, and let the Great Sea Serpent sink for the last time.

"The next day I heard that my father was sick, so I left in a hurry for home. I found father in bed.

" 'Hennery,' says he, when I got to his room, 'I have something to say to you alone, my son.' So the others left, and says he, 'Are you home for good, Hennery?'

" 'I reckon so,' says I.

" 'Through with your serpent now?'

" 'What do you mean, pa?' I said, feeling queer.

" 'Well, I saw the head you was making up in the toolhouse, my son, and I thought mebbe this was only a visit.' And sure enough, that old feller had knowed the whole thing, and never opened his mouth to a soul.

" 'Hennery,' he said after a minute, 'I've been thinkin' about you, my son. You didn't pay any attention to me; you left the farm when I needed you, and with me sick here this summer, your sister Maria has been the only dependence of the family. I can't live long, Hennery, and I've made a will givin' you the cottage and lot up on the road, and leavin' the house and farm to your sister, my son.' Well, he died a couple of months after that. Maria has the farm yet, and somehow I've"——

The old man stopped his story abruptly. A look of intense annoyance overspread his face. "Well, I swow," he ejaculated. "Sure as you live that fish has bit off bait, hook and all, and I never knowed it." Then after a moment's pause, he added, half resignedly, "Well, that's just like me; ever since '55 I've jest been agoin' to ketch a fish; never do."

The Twice Told Life of Thomas Dart.

Driven by a high autumn wind, the rain swept down Fifth Avenue in billowy sheets, forcing itself into doorways and crannies, and beating fiercely on every window-pane that faced the east.

Seen at long intervals through the driving rain, a few belated unfortunates were struggling up or down the avenue under the scanty and pitiful shelter of umbrellas tilted unavailingly against the storm.

A cab now and then rattled hurriedly by, as though driver and horse were both equally anxious to regain shelter.

On such a night the average mortal, however restless, elects to stay at home, and on this particular evening nearly all New York seemed to be of one mind.

Even the clubs were well nigh deserted, and in one of the larger ones there were but three members in the long, softly lighted library. They sat together by a broad window, that would have commanded a fine view of New York's most famous street had not the gusts of November wind driven the rain along the glass in little rivulets, which for minutes at a time shut out all the outside world except the prismatic glimmer of the electric lights—steadily glowing along the avenue in spite of wind and storm.

"A gloomy night conduces to gloomy thoughts," remarked the Doctor to his two companions. "I attended the funeral of a distant cousin of mine yesterday afternoon, and I've been thinking about the poor fellow off and on ever since."

"Especially sad case?" asked one of the others, sympathetically.

"No; it was not. There were few present at the funeral, and few, whether present or absent, to mourn that the poor fellow slept his last sleep. He was fifty-two years old when he died; a quiet, unobtrusive old bachelor; one of New York's great army of hall-bedroom boarders. He began life in this city as a bookkeeper, and when death came, twenty-seven years later, he had not moved. He was a bookkeeper still.

"We had nothing in common, and I seldom saw him, but after the services yesterday I began to look up his life, and it has haunted me ever since."

The Doctor paused.

"To think," he resumed after a moment's silence, "that a human being in the midst of civilization can pass from the cradle to the grave without leaving behind even the slightest impress, influence or incident is actually appalling. Did you ever trace an absolutely uneventful life from beginning to end?" he added, abruptly.

"To answer for myself, no," replied the younger of the Doctor's two companions. "All of us who are normally constituted desire to leave some imprint on the world, be it large or small, before we depart, and perhaps the normal mind recoils from its abnormal, ambitionless brother."

"Maybe you are right," said the Doctor, thoughtfully, looking out through the blurred window-pane. "The life of Thomas Dart was as stagnant as a millpond. I cannot shake off the memory of its utter failure.

"He came to New York in 1867. His early life had not been phenomenal. Most people would have called it uneventful, but youth is always the uneventful period. His parents were people of position, education and small resources. They had sent Tom to college as their extremest effort, and as he manifested no inclination toward a profession his father secured a chance for him as a bookkeeper in the business house of John Morton & Co., feeling that with his home training, his thorough education and good sense the making of his son's successful future lay in his own hands.

"The boy had many good qualities. He was likewise handicapped by some bad ones. He was a strong, active, handsome fellow, popular with all who knew him, possessing good habits and an excellent mental equipment. His besetting sin, and one which threatened fatal consequences to success in life, was a tendency to accept what the day brought forth, and to neither care nor plan for the future, indolently content to let events shape themselves.

"Attention to his new duties won the confidence of his superiors and an occasional pleasant word from the head of the firm. The first year was a busy, but not especially significant one.

"Like most young men of moderate resource he occupied a hall bedroom in a comfortable but inexpensive boarding-house, and his evenings were spent in careless but harmless ways.

"Times flies in the metropolis. Somehow it seems to move faster here than elsewhere. The country sleeps eight good hours of the twenty-four—sound, refreshing sleep, that wraps the whole community in its dreamless robe, but the city never sleeps. Its throb of life is unceasing. The myriad lights that glow to speed the setting sun are there to greet his coming.

"Two years vanished before careless Tom Dart

realized their passage. His position in the book-keeper's office had but slightly improved. Although well liked and respected, he seemed to lack that indefinable something which inspires confidence and brings promotion. A lack of alertness or, better stated, perhaps, a lack of ambition that should keep his mind ever fixed and ready to go ahead at full steam on demand seemed to blame for his failure to secure advancement. In business the man who does not expect advancement, and does not act as though he expected it, seldom gets it.

"And so Tom Dart settled slowly down into a rut. His daily routine accomplished, he felt too tired or too indolent to cultivate social chances. He neglected his father's friends, who had gladly opened their family circles to him, and they forgot him. He read in his hall bedroom, talked and smoked with the man at the other end of the hall, played whist at the inexpensive club which he had joined, and spent an occasional evening at the theatre.

" 'You've been with us three years, haven't you, Dart?' inquired Mr. Morton, pleasantly, one evening, as they happened to leave the office together.

" 'Yes, sir.'

" 'Don't forget, young man, that attention to duty must be supplemented by a constant watchfulness for chances to advance. Opportunities reach their fruition when they appear. Unaccepted they vanish.'

Tom respectfully assented.

That evening was one of much self-examination, and he resolved to make changes in his conduct.

" 'I believe you live in the city, don't you, Mr. Dart?' inquired the cashier of Tom, a few days afterward, as the business of the day was about over.

" 'Yes; Twenty-eighth street, near Fourth avenue,' replied the young bookkeeper.

" 'Will you do me the favor to take this package to Mr. Morton, and deliver it to him personally? He has gone home without it, and it contains some papers which require attention this evening. They are too valuable to trust to a messenger, and as he lives on Fifth Avenue near you, it will not be out of your way and will greatly oblige me.'

Tom expressed his entire willingness to be of service, and half an hour later rang the bell of Mr. Morton's handsome residence.

" 'Mr. Morton isn't at home,' said the servant, in answer to the bookkeeper's inquiry.

Tom hesitated. He could not leave the package, and did not wish to retain it.

A prettily dressed young girl was coming downstairs and had overheard his inquiry.

" 'My father is not to return until late, I be-

lieve. Is there anything I can do?' she asked,
stepping forward. 'I am Miss Morton.'

" 'Thank you,' said Tom, courteously. 'I have
a valuable package from the office for Mr. Morton, and was told to deliver it to him only, but,
of course, Miss Morton is a satisfactory substitute.'

" 'A safe one, anyway,' she replied, pleasantly, taking the envelope.

"Tom bowed and withdrew, but his dreams
that night were filled with pretty Marie Morton,
and it was several days before her image faded.

"Perhaps good-looking Tom Dart had remained
in Miss Marie's mind also, for one afternoon
in the following week Mr. Morton stopped at
Tom's desk and expressed his regret at not seeing him, adding a kindly invitation to call at his
house.

"The young bookkeeper was more than pleased
at the chance. 'I'll go next week,' he said, emphatically, to himself. But next week came and
went and Tom never made the call.

" 'I can't help it,' he said. 'I couldn't go anyway. My evening clothes are worn out, and I'd
be out of place. Of course Miss Marie is beautiful and accomplished, but I'd fall in love with
her and be miserable. What business have I,
Thomas Dart, bookkeeper, inhabiting one suit
of clothes and a hall bedroom, to think of her?
Mind your business, Tom. Smoke your pipe, be
comfortable, and stay where you belong.'

"Occasionally he saw his parents. They were older now, and needed more attention, but his visits were necessarily brief. His life in the city was monotonous, but Tom enjoyed it, and, after all, he was the most concerned. Moreover, he had a circle of friends. There were the Rosenbaums opposite. Not exactly Tom's style or class, if judged by the old days, but, then, the girls were awfully jolly; and Colonel Taxter, who had a bachelor apartment on the next block, and the Connelly's, just across Sixth Avenue. Of course he had friends. And between them all time ran tranquilly away—ran the faster because there was little to mark its passage.

" 'Five years to-day since I came here,' he remarked, one morning at the office, to the bookkeeper next to him.

" 'That so? You ought to ask for a raise.'

" 'I suppose I should,' rejoined Tom, 'but the woods are full of bookkeepers; they might bounce me.'

" 'All right,' said his neighbor, cheerfully, 'then I'd move up to your desk."

"They both laughed and resumed work. That was all the anniversary brought to Tom, and before he took time to think about it another had come and gone.

"Curious how fast the years sped away. Why notice the passage of a single paltry year in an uneventful life? Take them in twos and threes

and groups. Take them in their effects, for in
that alone is their passage apparent.

"The five years of Dart's service became multi-
plied by four.

"His parents were dead.

"Mr. Morton was dead. The old firm was now
the John Morton Company. The officers were
new men, and most of the clerks were new com-
ers also, but half a dozen veterans held on.
Among these Thomas Dart ranked high in years
of service.

"Mr. Dart was a middle-aged man, fairly well
preserved, but his hair was gray, his brow a bit
wrinkled, his form less erect. Life sentence to
hard living in a boarding-house had borne fruit
in slovenly appearance and decreased attention
to habits of polite living. A button off, collar
torn, coat threadbare and worn far beyond its
natural life. Symptoms, but unfailing ones.

" 'What's become of Dart?' asked a classmate
at the quarter-century reunion.

" 'Just where he was twenty years ago,' answered another, 'growing old and standing
still. The man in the parable buried his talent.
Dart didn't even do that. He laid it down just
where it was given to him, and the wind and
rain and snow and sun beat on it, and it
weathered and crumbled and blew away.'

"There remained to Thomas Dart the habits
of his earlier years. The future with its wealth

of possibility, which is the birthright of every
young man, was his no longer. The expecta-
tions of a home, a family and a fair degree of
prosperity, which all men ought to cherish and
most men realize, had long ago faded below his
mental horizon. Thought, hope and wish had
contracted; habits narrowed. The boarders
thought Mr. Dart was prosy. Only a few more
years were needed to make him a slippered,
white-headed bore.

"Why trace the change?

"The infinite possibilities of a human life had
blossomed and died. The wilted leaf of existence alone remained, withering and useless.
Why watch it disappear?

———

"The general manager came out of his private
office with a telegram in his hand.

" 'Mr. Dunnell,' he said, gravely, to the head
bookkeeper, 'I have sad news for you. Our Mr.
Dart died this morning at 7 o'clock.'

" 'I am distressed to hear it, sir.'

" 'I knew you would be. He was an old and
trusted clerk.'

"The cashier joined the little group that had
gathered at the news. 'Dart came here three
years after me,' he said, sadly. 'He had twenty-seven years of service to his credit in this
house. I have thirty.'

" 'With the difference,' said the general manager, 'that he was always a routine man. You never were.'

" 'How old was he?' asked a young bookkeper.

"The cashier meditated 'Dart was not an old man,' he said. 'I suppose he was about fifty-three.'

" 'Was he married?' asked a new clerk.

" 'No; he never seemed to have any matrimonial inclinations.'

" 'Very sad,' commented the head bookkeeper, mentally considering which of the younger men to advance to Dart's place. 'I did not know he was seriously ill. He was here last Tuesday. We had better order flowers,' he added, 'and appoint a committee to attend the funeral.'

" 'Certainly,' said the general manager. 'And, Mr. Dunnell, I think we won't fill Mr. Dart's place just now. We can get on very well. Just divide up his work among the others. He was not a necessity.'

"Two days later a little company gathered at the funeral. There was not even crape on the door. The landlady objected. She said it made the house look dismal for the other boarders.

"Another day, and Thomas Dart slept beside his parents in the inland city of his birth. His sister had come on to be with him at the end. She tenderly gathered up her brother's few simple belongings and transferred them to her own distant home.

"That was all.

"Another life had come, matured and vanished unnoticed.

"Seemingly not even an atom of strength had gone out of the hem of the great world's garment.

"On the mighty tides of sorrow, joy, business, pleasure and suffering there was not a ripple to mark the passing of Thomas Dart, dead."

The Doctor paused, much affected. His two friends made no effort to break the silence. Rain had ceased for the moment, and the wind was sweeping down the deserted avenue with redoubled fury. The long line of lights twinkled sharply beneath its influence.

"That is the life of Thomas Dart as he lived it," continued the Doctor, quietly. "No power can change it now, but last night I lay awake and thought about him, and it seemed to me that if he had only done something, traded horses, speculated—anything to break his lifetime of monotony—I could have forgiven him, and so, for my own satisfaction, I constructed a fictitious Dart; made him speculate—for speculation generally depends on luck, not brains. I made the fictitious Dart succeed in life, and yet so narrow is the line between success and failure that the only difference between Dart, failure, and Dart, success, was that I gave the latter a push at the right moment. He merely accepted opportunities instead of declining them."

"Let us have the fictitious Dart, Doctor," remarked Bradley. "You owe him to us," he added, emphatically, "as some compensation for the gloomy reality."

"Fiction is a poor match for truth in any contest," said the Doctor, "but you are welcome to my successful Dart. I made the turning point in his life come just after his employer gave him that kindly bit of advice."

" 'Dart,' remarked a young broker who lived on the floor below him in the commonplace uptown boarding-house, as they sat at the dinner-table together the next evening, 'have you any money to invest?'

" 'Mighty little, why?' asked Tom, with languid interest.

" 'I don't want to talk shop,' replied his friend, 'and even to a customer I seldom offer advice, but as a friend I want to tell you there is an opportunity just now for money making in stocks that comes only once or twice in ten years, and I thought I might do you a service.'

" 'Of course,' continued the broker, as he folded his napkin and pushed back from the table, at which he and Tom alone remained, 'of course there never was any speculation of any kind that was absolutely safe. It would not be speculation if it was.'

"In Tom's trunk there was an envelope containing $100. It represented his savings from a small salary with a still smaller ability to save. His inclination was to keep it there and take no risks, but the advice of his employer flashed across his mind. 'My tendency,' he said to himself, 'is always to hang back and I am making no progress in any direction. If I lose my $100 I am not vitally affected. If I make money in the transaction I may be able to better myself materially.'

" 'If you satisfy me you are right,' said Tom, aloud, 'I will invest a small amount.'

"Thereupon his friend sketched the prevailing conditions in the market; the rise and fall of values and their effect, especially upon one stock, which seemed to have been overlooked, but was now apparently on the verge of a sharp upward movement.

"Tom was convinced. The next morning he called at his friend's office, deposited with him his $100, and arranged the details of the purchase.

"He was in a feverish condition that day, far removed from his usual careless state of mind, and he watched anxiously for closing hour, and the afternoon paper obtainable with it. Turning to the financial column he saw, with burning cheeks, that his friend's predictions were more than realized. There had been a sharp advance in the market, and he, Thomas Dart, clerk, by the doubling-up process his friend recommended, possessed, with principal and profit, over $800.

" 'Well, Dart,' his broker friend said that evening as Tom greeted him, 'It's a pleasure to see the market come your way, but I've got one piece of advice to give you in sober earnest. Don't squander a cent and don't lose your head. You have made a beginning in the way of capital which you can build up further with caution, but keep your head.'

"Tom did not go to the club that evening. He told a friend who called for him that he had a business matter to attend to, the first personal business that had afflicted Thomas Dart since his arrival in the metropolis.

"The result of his consideration was to begin a new and cautious transaction, but with double the amount of the former one, which had been closed.

"It so happened that the moment was ripe for the three transactions which Tom made in the ensuing few days, and within two weeks he had to his credit the sum of $2,000.

" 'I am through,' he said, emphatically, to his friend.

" 'And by stopping you show more head than most men,' remarked the other. 'To know when to stop, and stop there, is half of success.'

"The two weeks that had passed had been intensely anxious ones for Dart, but they had worked a mighty change in him, which, with the success he had attained, became almost a revolution.

"Tom felt like another man himself, and the change was decidedly noticeable to others. He displayed redoubled energy at the office, and the head bookkeeper remarked to the cashier that Dart was becoming a valuable man. He seemed to take genuine interest in his work.

" 'You surprise me,' said the other. 'I always liked Dart, but he appeared to me too lazy to succeed.'

" 'He's all nerves and energy now,' rejoined the head bookkeeper.

" 'Dart,' said the cashier a few evenings later, as the clerks were leaving, 'I wonder if I can impose on you for an important errand uptown. You live in the city, do you not?'

" 'Yes, sir; but that would not signify. I should be at your service, anyway.'

" 'Thank you,' replied the cashier, pleased at his response, and recalling the head bookkeeper's remark. 'I have an exceedingly valuable package for Mr. Morton. He has forgotten to take it with him, and must have it to-night. I do not dare to trust it to a messenger, and you can do me a great service by putting it in his hands.'

"Tom buttoned the precious envelope securely up in his coat and hurried uptown.

" 'Perhaps there is an opportunity here,' he said, and, stopping at his own room, which was within a few blocks of Mr. Morton's Fifth Avenue residence, he made himself thoroughly presentable, and with little delay rang the bell of his employer's handsome house.

" 'Mr. Morton is not at home,' said the servant, in response to his inquiry.

"Dart hesitated. He could not retain the package, and yet he surely could not give it to a servant.

"A prettily dressed girl was descending the stairs as Tom had made his inquiry.

" 'My father is not expected home until late,' she said, coming forward. 'Is there anything I can do for you? I am Miss Morton.'

" 'I have some important papers from the office for Mr. Morton, to be intrusted to no one but himself. In his absence, however, I am sure Miss Morton is a satisfactory substitute.'

" 'Reliable, anyway,' she answered, smiling, with the least bit of admiration in her glance. Tom made an attractive picture as he stood in the doorway—handsome, well-dressed and well-bred.

"He placed the package in Miss Morton's hands, bowed courteously and was gone.

"In no such brief way, however, did he dis-

miss the memory of Miss Marie Morton. She
was the heroine of many a daydream and the
inspiration for his new-found ambitions.

" 'Who was the young clerk, John, that called
here last night with a package for you?' asked
Mrs. Morton, at the breakfast-table, the morning after Dart's errand. 'Marie was quite impressed with his youth and beauty,' she added,
laughingly.

" 'Potter or Fellows, from the cashier's office,
I suppose,' replied Mr. Morton. 'Neither one is
beautiful nor remarkable,' he added.

"Miss Marie looked indignant.

" 'I said the man was a gentleman and good
looking, that was all,' she protested, 'and it's
true, whether it was Potter or Fellows or somebody else.'

" 'Potter has red chin whiskers,' continued
her father, with some amusement, 'and Fellows has nothing in particular except a pair of
ears as big as griddle-cakes. I should not back
either one of them in a beauty show, but, then, a
man can't judge of his own sex. Maybe they
are both beautiful.'

"The recollection of the breakfast-table chat
crossed Mr. Morton's mind that afternoon at
the office.

" 'Whom did you send up to my house last
evening?' he inquired of the cashier.

" 'Dart, sir.'

" 'Dart!' repeated Mr. Morton, in surprise. 'I
did not suppose he lingered long enough after
closing-hour to be available for such an errand.'

" 'Dart is doing very well, sir,' replied the
cashier. 'The head of his department tells me
that he has completely changed within the last
month, and promises to be one of his most valuable men.'

"Mr. Morton found opportunity before leaving
to stop at Tom's desk.

" 'I was sorry not to see you last evening,
Dart,' he said, in his kindly way. 'Mrs. Morton and my daughter will be at home until June,
and I should be glad to have you call upon us.'

"The young bookkeeper thanked his employer
heartily, and decided to take early advantage
of the invitation.

" Tom Dart's thoughts, however, were not all
of sentiment. His capital was deposited to his
credit in one of the larger banks, and he was
seriously considering his next step.

" 'This is a matter of head,' he said to himself. 'If I make few missteps I have the foun-
dation of independence. I want no more stocks.
I have had my success there. The next result
would be failure. I want no schemes. They are
all right for men without capital or with a great
amount of it.'

"By this process of elimination he found himself reduced to real estate, and he at length de-

cided to buy one or two lots, build a house and sell it. Accordingly his spare time was spent in searching for an available and satisfactory site. This accomplished, he made his cash purchase the means of obtaining a low price, borrowed money on mortgages and began the erection of a dainty cottage. Before it was completed he had found a purchaser, and had handsomely increased his capital.

"This gave him an opportunity to purchase two other small pieces of property that he had noticed favorably, and he began the repetition of his successful building venture.

"His personal life had completely changed. Improved work at the office had brought advancement, and Tom had removed to an inexpensive bachelor apartment, which his mother had aided him to make homelike and attractive. The club was forgotten. Tom was a man of business. The effect was noticeable in his improved appearance and bearing. His manners, and even his clothing, showed the change.

"Twice Tom had called at Mr. Morton's house. He had been most kindly received, and his own impressions of Miss Morton had been renewed and strengthened, but serious thoughts in that direction were of course presumptuous.

"Time passes quickly in the metropolis and five years have gone.

"Tom Dart's capital, in spite of one or two

reverses, now amounted to $5,000. At the office he was assistant to the head bookkeeper and would probably succeed that worthy some day, but Dart was conscious of a growing discontent. He had demonstrated his own ability to succeed outside of the routine of the counting-room, and for more than a year he had continued in Mr. Morton's employ solely to accumulate a sum of ready money sufficient to live on for one year without employment, during which time he figured that he could nurse his real estate enterprises into profitable and self-supporting realities.

"Another potent cause of discontent came from the heart. Wisely or unwisely, he had permitted himself to fall deeply in love with his employer's daughter. Unwise it undoubtedly was if his chances of success were the sole consideration, but this attachment had many times formed a welcome reinforcement to Tom's wearied ambition, and spurred him on to renewed or increased effort.

"As an employe of Mr. Morton, however, he saw no prospect of anything like actual equality in spite of the cordial welcome he always received. He felt that he must be able to come to the house as an outsider, an independent business man, at least fairly successful, and welcome for his own qualities.

"Matters were approaching a crisis, when

Thomas Dart was summoned one morning in June to Mr. Morton's private office. 'Mr. Dart,' said his employer, seriously, 'We are about to make a most important and radical change in this business. I have sold my interest to a syndicate of business men younger in years than I, and they are about to form a corporation with large capital to conduct it. The details are now complete, and will take effect the first of next month. I have sent for you to tell you that I urged your appointment as head bookkeeper with advanced salary, but one of the new proprietors has a man for the place, and my request was not granted. I wish to express my own regard for you and my appreciation of your work. Your present position is doubtless secure, but I am sorry you will obtain no advancement.'

" 'Let me thank you, sir, for your kind efforts,' said Tom earnestly, 'and your still kinder words, but your announcement brings to a point a plan I have been maturing for some months and have hesitated to carry out. I have been fortunate enough, by profitable real estate investments, to develop my savings into a considerable property. I believe I can make far more by devoting my time to real estate enterprises than I can in the counting-room, and therefore, with your retirement, I shall resign also, for that,' added Tom, skilfully, 'relieves me of my only regret.'

"Mr. Morton had heard his employe's statement with much surprise.

" 'Do you own real estate now,' he asked, incredulously, 'or are you about to acquire it?'

" 'I own four houses, sir, two in Yorkville, one in the suburbs of Brooklyn, and one in Orange. They are valued at about $20,000, and are mortgaged for $14,000. I said four houses,' added Tom, 'I should say three, for I think I have sold the Brooklyn house, and as it is empty I am especially fortunate. The others are rented and paying well.'

" 'You have greatly surprised me, Mr. Dart,' said his employer, rising. 'You have proved to me that you possess qualities I did not attribute to you, and if I were to remain in business I should make it an object for you to stay with me in a responsible position. As it is, remember you are always welcome socially at my house. Mrs. Morton and my daughter are going abroad this month for the summer, but we shall be at home next winter as usual.'

"Tom's resolution was made instantly. 'Your decision gives me the chance for a hurried trip to Europe myself, this summer,' he said. 'I have longed to go, and had almost given up hope of it.'

"Already the evidence of Tom's ability and success had made a change in Mr. Morton's manner and attitude toward his whilom employe. 'Do you really propose to go?' he inquired.

" 'I do indeed, sir.'

" 'When ?'

" 'Some time this month,' hazarded Tom, not deeming it necessary to explain that he must first learn when and by what line Mrs. Morton and Miss Marie were to sail.

" 'My family go over alone,' continued Mr. Morton, thoughtfully, 'for I shall be detained here another month, and am to meet them in Paris in August. I have worried somewhat at their crossing unattended. I wonder if you could not arrange as a particular favor to take the same steamer and go over with them?'

"Tom Dart could hardly believe his ears. 'I should be delighted to make the passage in their company, Mr. Morton,' he said, 'and I am still more pleased to be able to serve you.'

"And so it happened that when a certain Cunard steamer sailed from New-York in late June, 1873, it bore among its passengers Mrs. Morton, Miss Marie Morton and Mr. Thomas Dart.

"Miss Morton's attitude toward the devoted and good-looking young man in whose care she and her mother had been placed was that of a friend. Mrs. Morton seemed unable to forget that Mr. Dart was, or had long been, a book-keeper in her husband's employ, and though kindly and courteous, she permitted no approach to intimacy. It was different with Miss Marie. She was a bright, good-looking and singularly unaffected girl, and Tom had always been a favorite from their first meeting. She now found him a delightful companion. He seemed to think of her comfort only, and was devotedly, but not obtrusively attentive.

"The voyage over was not eventful, but Tom would not have rendered that verdict. He planned after landing to devote a few weeks to a hurried trip through England and Scotland and then to return to America.

"Reluctant, however, to part with the Mortons, he decided at Mrs. Morton's suggestion, to remain with them during their stay in London.

"The elder lady's motive was a double one. She had early discovered that the young bookkeeper's attentions were too earnest and continuous to be a mere matter of duty. She also thought she saw some encouragement in her daughter's manner and actions, and the latter impression was a source of much uneasiness and anxiety. Mrs. Morton had her own plans for her daughter, and they did not include the young bookkeeper. Her first idea was to part company with Tom at Liverpool, and so decisively that he would not be seen again during the trip, but the approach to a strange land brought with it a dread of travelling unattended, and she was compelled to admit that Tom was a model traveller. She concluded, moreover, that it would be better to encourage his presence with them

for a few days longer, merely to let the cruel
separation which wealth and position enforce
perform its blighting task. The formalities that
vanish on shipboard quickly reappear on land.
Marie would see the wide gulf between herself
and Mr. Dart, and he would perceive the folly of
aspiring to the hand of his employer's daughter.
Accordingly on arriving in London Mrs. Morton chose the most expensive accommodations,
determined to set a pace which her husband's
altogether too gentlemanly clerk could not equal.

"By a kindly good fortune, however, Tom's
Brooklyn real estate transaction had been cleared
up profitably before he left New-York. He was,
therefore, well supplied with money, and Mrs.
Morton was surpried and annoyed to find her
escort retaining quarters fully equal to hers, as
a matter of course, and instead of being overwhelmed by the usages of polite society when
politest, Tom Dart was so well-bred and fault-
lessly dressed that he made a far more attractive appearance than most of the fashionable
young Americans whom they met.

"All of which was quite unimportant to Tom.
He was watchful of appearances and determined
to lose nothing on that score, but beyond that
Marie was his only thought, and he contrived
innumerable little excursions and trips that
would give him more of her society. To her
mother's annoyance and increasing alarm, Miss

Marie seemed to prefer Tom and his daily plans to the elder lady's more fashionable programmes.

"The last day of their first week in London was marked by an incident that intensified Mrs. Morton's annoyance. A party of wealthy and exclusiveBostonians had just arrived. Tom was now so dangerous that he must be disposed of, for her theories were evidently all wrong, and she merely awaited the arrival of her friends to form a convenient pretext for disposing of her escort; but to Mrs. Morton's disgust two members of the party proved to be college friends of Tom's, and greeted him with delight.

"That was the last and most aggravating annoyance, and she decided to end it promptly.

" 'What are your plans, Mr. Dart?' she asked pleasantly that evening.

" 'For to-morrow, Mrs. Morton?'

" 'Well, no, in general, now that you have located us so pleasantly in London.'

" 'Oh, I have no particular plans. Perhaps I may go up to the Scotch lakes in a week or ten days.'

" 'I was beginning to fear, Mr. Dart,' continued Mrs. Morton, in especially pleasant tones, 'that we were imposing on your kindness, and keeping you in London against your own inclination. Now that the Rhodes are here, we shall have an increasing number of friends. So pray feel at liberty to leave us at any moment you please.

You have been so attentive to our wants, and have been such a useful escort, especially to my daughter, that we are both more than grateful. The financial part can be reimbursed readily, the personal part cannot, and I can only thank you most earnestly.' The words and tone were studiedly courteous, but there was no mistaking the inference.

"Tom said nothing. He bowed coldly and withdrew. She had made hideously plain at length the financial distance that separated him, Thomas Dart, from the girl he loved.

"Tom's best efforts at the theatre that evening, were not satisfactory to Miss Marie.

" 'What is the matter, Mr. Dart?' she inquired during the intermission, as Tom seemed unable to recall the principal character in the first act. 'Are you sick, or bored?' she asked.

" 'Neither, Miss Morton. I am sad.'

" 'That is worse than either of my suggestions. Whence does it arise? Indigestion?'

" 'I am going back to the United States day after to-morrow,' said Dart quietly.

"Marie's cheek paled slightly.

" 'Why do you go?' she asked after a moment's silence.

" 'One reason is because my business needs me.'

" 'Then that is only one reason of several, Mr. Dart?' The resumption of the play prevented further conversation. Miss Morton heard as little of the dialogue of the second act as her companion did of the first.

" 'I want to know the other reasons,' she whispered as Dart helped the two ladies into their carriage after the play was over.

" 'I'm afraid I cannot tell you,' replied Tom sadly.

"The next day he announced to Mrs. Morton that a business matter of importance recalled him to America; that he had abandoned his trip to Scotland in consequence, and would catch the earliest steamer.

"The farewell with Marie was not so easily accomplished. Her usual unaffected cordiality was gone, and Tom found a quiet, well-bred, self-possessed young woman. His own high-spirited nature responded to the chill of the parting with an added chill, and their frank and pleasant intercourse seemed to have suddenly become all constraint.

"The last thanks were spoken by mother and daughter, the last farewell said. Tom bowed himself out of their parlor and started aimlessly down the corridor.

" 'Mr. Dart,' said a familiar voice.

"He turned hastily.

" 'We expect you to call upon us after we return to New-York. Will you not?'

It had not escaped Dart that Mrs. Morton had

omitted the usual invitation. He felt that the omission was intentional, as, indeed, it was.

" 'Do you wish me to come, Miss Morton?' he asked.

" 'Oh, I am not particular,' she said demurely.

" 'Then why do you invite me?'

" 'Papa will be glad to see you.'

"Tom was very close to her. Somehow the constraint was all gone.

" 'Is he the only one who would welcome me, Miss Morton? After the pleasant hours we have spent together on sea and land, I had hoped that—that we were at least good friends.'

" 'I hope we are Mr. Dart.'

" 'Certainly I shall never call at your home again, Miss Morton,' said Tom gravely, 'unless your invitation represents your own wish that I should come.'

The color suddenly rushed to Marie's face.

" 'Please come,' she said half glancing at the handsome young fellow before her, 'and besides I have something to say to you when you call.'

" 'Can't you say it now?' asked Tom, eagerly.

" 'Not possibly."

" 'Is it important?'

"Marie pulled a leaf or two out of the rose she was wearing, and meditated. 'That depends on circumstances, Mr. Dart, and possibly I might not tell you after all.'

" 'Don't say that,' pleaded Tom.

" 'Then you must promise to call,'

" 'Indeed I do promise.'

" 'There is one other condition, Mr. Dart,' she added severely.

" 'I agree in advance, Miss Morton.'

" 'You must be exceedingly nice,' and with a smile that Tom cherished all the way across the Atlantic, and she was gone.

"The voyage allowed Tom Dart plenty of time to consider his affairs in every light, and lay out a plan of action.

"There was a strong inclination at times toward the old, indolent, careless way of life, but the incentive to action was so great that Tom looked eagerly forward to an energetic and sensible campaign. He decided to get down to business without a day's delay, in order to have definite plans by early fall. The Mortons were to return in September, and Tom was especially anxious to have some results secured by that time, for he early decided that he would make his feelings known to Miss Marie at the first opportunity. With these resolutions uppermost Tom Dart, bronzed, hearty and well dressed, left the steamer and plunged into the busy throng of commercial New York.

"The three months that followed seemed to pass with more than ordinary rapidity, and Tom had scarcely awakened to the fact that autumn had come when he met Miss Morton on Broadway one afternoon in late September.

" 'You were actually rushing by without seeing me at all,' she said, indignantly, as Tom wheeled joyously around and joined her.

" 'Impossible,' he said, solemnly. 'I should have seen you, or known you were near, even if I were two blocks away.'

" 'Nonsense, Mr. Dart. Friends don't have affinities like that. You know we agreed in London that we actually were friends.'

" 'A knowledge, Miss Morton, that has been pleasanter to me than any other recollection of our trip.'

" 'We only returned last week,' continued Marie, 'and already papa is deep in some new business plans. We thought he had retired permanently, but he says he must have occupation.'

"The short walk to the Morton residence was covered all too soon for Tom, and he lingered at the steps.

" 'Please come in and dine with us, Mr. Dart,' said Marie, heartily. 'Mamma is in Stockbridge and papa and I are alone. Moreover, I am sure he wants to see you, for yesterday he inquired your address.'

"Thus urged, Tom accepted, and was heartily welcomed by Mr. Morton, who invited him to his library when dinner was over.

" 'The fact is, Dart,' he remarked as he lighted a cigar, 'I cannot keep out of active work of one kind or another, and several of us have lately

organized a company to handle trust money and
real estate. I thought immediately of you in
connection with it. How are you progressing?'

"Tom explained his affairs, and an hour later,
when he arose to go, he had been offered and had
accepted an official position in the new company
at an ample salary.

" 'I presume my daughter thinks I have stolen
her guest,' said Mr. Morton, smiling, as Tom bid
him good night. 'You will find her in the rear
parlor, if you do not mind making my apologies.'
Tom was entirely willing. He had some remarks of his own to make.

"The door of the back parlor was partly open,
the light burned low, and Marie was playing
softly on the piano.

"She turned as Tom entered. 'Time is almost
up, Mr. Dart,' she said.

"Tom began his apologies.

" 'Oh, you need not apologize,' she interrupted.
'To a man the plea of business is ever new and
ever unanswerable. I know all about it. A
man meets another man, and they smoke, tell
jokes and completely forget engagements or
duties, and when confronted by their short-
comings they look solemn and fall back on "business," for business covereth all things. Men,
Mr. Dart, are one and all deceitful creatures,
and, also, you are no better than your sex.'
Which freed Marie's mind and she resumed playing.

"Tom was standing a few feet from the piano. He had never seen her look so attractive. A gown of some soft, clinging silk was wondrously becoming to her slender, girlish figure, dark hair and black eyes. It was almost joy enough to be alone with her in the quiet lamp-lighted room, even though her greeting was a lecture.

"'Miss Morton,' said Tom, impetuously, 'your father and I have been talking business, and I have this evening reached conclusions that will affect my whole future life, but I can truthfully tell you that there was not a moment of the whole time when I would not have hurried to you, had I consulted my own inclinations.'

"Tom's face was very near her as he leaned on the piano.

"The conversation had grown suddenly personal. Miss Morton made no reply. Her hands wandered gently over the keys in Rubinstein's Melodie.

"'I'll forgive you,' she said, looking up brightly a few moments later.

"'Turn up the light, Mr. Dart, and be seated. I have some photographs to show you.'

"Tom did not move.

"'You have something to tell me, Miss Morton,' he said.

"'I have?'

"'Yes. Don't you recall our parting in London?'

" 'Indeed I do, and I recall the condition attached to my remark.'

" 'Have I not complied with it?' asked Tom anxiously.

"Marie arose with mock solemnity.

" 'How can you ask such a question,' she inquired, 'when I have actually been obliged to lecture you for neglect?'

" 'And you won't tell me, Miss Morton?'

" 'Not to-night.'

" 'Suppose I call soon again, on purpose for it,' suggested the artful Dart.

" 'It might not do any good.'

" 'Why?'

" 'I may never tell you.'

" 'Miss Morton,' said Tom, impulsively, 'I have something to say to you. Unlike your "something," it cannot wait. It may not interest you, but it is all important to me.

" 'Ever since that night when I called here to see your father, and Providence brought you instead, you have been my ideal, my hope, my ambition. All my efforts have been but to deserve you.'

"Marie stood by the piano with hands clasped and eyes downcast.

"Tom was very close to her.

" 'Ever since that night in the hall,' he continued gently, 'I have loved you, and when I knew you better and saw you daily I loved you

184

more and more for your own good qualities. As for myself, Marie, I'm only an ordinary young fellow, who has made a little place for himself in the world, and for whom all of life and happiness depend on your loving him, though only a little, in return.'

" 'I don't think you are just to yourself, Mr. Dart,' said Marie, without looking up.

" 'Why?'

" 'You are not an "ordinary young fellow," judged by my standard,' and then raising her dark eyes to Tom's with a woman's first spoken love in their depths she whispered, 'for you are the dearest man in the world to me.'

"That was enough for Tom.

" 'What were you going to say to me, Marie?' he asked half an hour later. 'Have I not the right to hear now?'

" 'I said I might never tell you,' she said, 'and that it all depended on circumstances, anyway, didn't I?'

" 'You did, and worried me all the way across the Atlantic.'

"Marie laughed. 'I've said it already,' she said, blushing. 'You see I thought you liked me, and I knew I liked you, and so under proper circumstances'—Marie hid her face on Tom's shoulder —'what I had to say was—yes.'

"That was twenty years ago," concluded the Doctor, reflectively. "The middle-aged handsome, prosperous New Yorker whom you passed at Twenty-third street and Fifth avenue this afternoon was Thomas Dart, man of wealth, position and influence in this big community. The well-built young fellow with him was his oldest son."

The Doctor paused, and lighted the cigar which, neglected, had gone out.

"Your theoretical Dart, Doctor," said Bradley, heartily, "is a great success. We shall all sleep the better for him."

"There is only one trouble with Dart, happy, prosperous and married," rejoined his friend sadly.

"What is that?" asked Bradley.

The Doctor arose, buttoned up his coat and pushed back his chair.

"The story is totally false," he said.

www.ingramcontent.com/pod-product-compliance
Lightning Source LLC
Chambersburg PA
CBHW020537270326
41927CB00006B/623